Odd Men In

ODD MEN IN

A GALLERY OF CRICKET ECCENTRICS

A. A. THOMSON
Introduction by Leo Cooper

THE PAVILION LIBRARY

First published in Great Britain 1958

First published in the Pavilion Library in 1985 by
Pavilion Books Limited
196 Shaftesbury Avenue, London WC2H 8JL
in association with Michael Joseph Limited
44 Bedford Square, London WC1B 3DU

ISBN 0 907516 86 6
ISBN 0 907516 73 4 paperback

Printed and bound in Great Britain by
Billing & Sons Limited, Worcester

INTRODUCTION

I REMEMBER reading this book with great enjoyment when it was first published in 1958. I was already familiar with A. A. Thomson's writing, having been brought up in Yorkshire, for many of his articles appeared in various Yorkshire publications, as they did in *The Cricketer*. It is thus a pleasure for me to write an Introduction to what has always been one of my favourite cricket books.

Cricket, more than any other sport, has always produced a large number of eccentrics. This is partly, I suspect, because there is more time available during the course of each game to develop eccentricities. But equally the very nature of the game tacitly encourages great individuality. It is sad to reflect, though, that there seem to be fewer eccentrics about in the game today. I think they began to disappear round about the time that the distinction between Gentlemen and Players was abolished. Where are the Graces, the Hornbys, the Barlows, the Emmott Robinsons and the Wilfred Rhodeses now? Who behaves as imperiously as once did Lord Hawke? Who draws the crowds as did 'Croucher' Jessop, Johnnie Wardle with his rolling gait or Doug Wright with his astonishing action? Who excites comment as such players as Milburn, Alletson, Gleeson, or Gubby Allen used to? And what about Robert Montague Poore? During the 1899 season he became the most prolific run-scorer in England. In two months between 12 June and 12 August he scored 1,399 runs for Hampshire at an average of 116.58, including seven centuries. In fact in twenty-one innings that season he made 1,551 runs at an average of 91.23. And yet he did not take cricket that seriously. He was a brilliant swordsman, a fine polo player and also won the West of India lawn tennis championship. He was a fine shot too. He is said to have claimed that he never really took cricket to heart until he went out to India as a subaltern in the 7th Hussars. He also claimed that he learnt his cricket from text books. Of all the people in the history of the game he seems to stand for the Eccentric Ideal. He died in 1938. Well I suppose there is always Boycott to fall back on now, but he does not have much of a supporting cast. Not much of swordsman either!

In my playing days in club cricket I certainly came across a great many unusual characters, and indeed in my family we were brought up to believe that eccentricity was to be admired rather than disdained. My Great-aunt Maud was a case in point. She was, as far as we can ascertain, the first Lady member of Yorkshire County Cricket Club. She was all of six feet tall and, as you might suspect, had a passion for cricket. She also had a passion for Maurice Leyland, the great but diminutive Yorkshire left-hander, whom she bombarded with fan letters, some of which I still have. What a pair they would have made if they had ever got to the altar, or indeed the wicket. Aunt Maud left me all her cricket books when she died, and it was from them and from my father that I learnt all about the great players of the past and their characteristics, pecadillos, achievements and behaviour. One of these books was called *Bat & Ball*, edited by Thomas Moult and published in 1935. It contained a marvellous chapter at the beginning called 'The Story of the Game' and went on to describe the great characters of old such as Felix, Alfred Mynn, Fuller Pilch, 'The first of the Modern Giants', William Clarke, 'Captain of All England', F. R. Spofforth, 'Australia's Demon Bowler', and William Lillywhite, 'the pioneer of modern bowling'. How they all must be revolving in their graves today.

My father's greatest cricket story relates to The Hon. Lionel Tennyson and his famous innings in the 1923 Leeds Test Match against the Australians, who were spearheaded by that great fast bowling pair Gregory and Macdonald. Tennyson came in one evening when the fast men were at their most dangerous. He had injured his hand but he managed to remain not out overnight. The next day he completed a brilliant innings of 63 using only one hand. This unusual innings is still remembered vividly today by those who saw it. What many people do not know, though, is how Tennyson managed it. Some years ago now I was at a dinner party with the great man's son. We got to talking about the innings and he told me that on the morning after the injury his father had got up early and gone to a sports shop in Leeds and bought a prep-school sized bat which enabled him to use one hand only with greater facility. But, however it was achieved, the feat must remain in the cricket annals as one of the most remarkable innings of all time.

One of the players I would love to have watched was G. H. Simpson-Hayward of Worcestershire, the last lob bowler in first-class cricket, who faded from the scene in 1910. I did myself have the privilege of playing against a lob bowler in a club match in the late 1950s when, at Oakham in Rutland, the Yorkshire Gentlemen faced the Leicestershire Gentlemen. I don't remember the bowler's name – he was a bit long in the tooth but he was devilishly difficult to play, and his bowling was treated by all with great respect. And another great character against whom and with whom I played on many occasions was the redoubtable I. A. W. Gilliatt of Oxford University and Kent, reckoned by some to be the worst wicketkeeper ever to play for Kent (unless you count A. W. Catt who, playing for Kent against Northants in 1955, let through 48 byes in an innings). I. A.W. Gilliatt coached me at school. He was a man of enormous girth but with the greatest sense of cricket lore and manners. He bestrode any field on which he played like a colossus. He complained about the umpires, about the way the opposition were dressed, about behaviour in the pavilion, about the groundsmen, and indeed about anything that took his fancy, and yet he was a formidable opponent and a wonderful man to have on one's own side. He was very difficult to get out – you could never see the wicket – and few umpires had the courage either to resist his own appeals behind the wicket or accede to those against him in front of it. And yet he taught us all we knew. He loved the game and its players with a fierce passion and, although we regarded him as a huge (literally) joke, we lived in awe of him. He was a very kind man too. I still have a telegram, the pencil now fading, which he sent to my parents announcing my first hundred, for Radley against Eastbourne, in 1952. After the game he took the whole side out to dinner (including Bert, our pro) at the Trocadero – an event which was rendered possible when he told us that if we could beat Eastbourne by 4.20 we could catch an earlier train and dine at his expense, and of course we did.

There is little room in the modern first-class game for characters. There is too much at stake now. A man like Ray East can play it for laughs, perhaps; Botham can make jokes and get away with it, as can Graham Gooch; but on the whole the game at the top level has to be taken very seriously. Even at club level one no longer finds characters like Len Phillips of the BBC, who batted in pebble thick glasses and never wore batting gloves or a box and yet had an eye like a hawk; or Dr C. B. Clarke the great West Indian leg-spinner who, having spent some time as a guest of Her Majesty, re-appeared on the scene after his release the same as ever and continued to weave his spells over a host of club cricketers. And then there was the legendary Oliver Battcock, who for many years *was* 'The Incogniti', or his colleague 'Bush' Callaghan who was known to play cricket virtually every day of the season and never failed to score 2,000 runs, even flying to out-of-the-way places in late September to make sure that he could accumulate the vital missing runs. Once he lost his diary and the whole cricket club world was flung into a panic as they tried to recall if he was playing for them, and where, in response to his frantic requests.

Re-reading this book, I suppose it is true to say that it could not be written again, which is sad. Of the characters with whom A. A. Thomson deals only Fred Trueman is still with us in the game, although no longer playing – which allows me to finish by telling one the many stories, probably apocryphal, about him. Playing against one of the Universities, he clean bowled one of the undergraduates with a real beauty. As the youth passed Trueman on his way back to the pavilion the youth said, 'Well bowled, Mr Trueman, that was a beautiful ball,' to which Fred is alleged to have replied, 'Aye and it was bloody wasted on Thee.' I don't think this book will be wasted on anyone.

London, 1985   Leo Cooper

Contents

CHAPTER 1

The Eccentric Idea

I

In writing of eccentricity in cricketers, or indeed in anybody else, it might be helpful to discover what is meant by the expression. I say *might*, because definition is not always so easy. When I was a lad, my elders always counselled me to consult the dictionary and the *Thesaurus* for the meaning of any particular word. (Oh, my Nuttall and my Roget long ago. . . .) I usually found that the dictionary told you too little and the *Thesaurus* told you too much. The adjective *eccentric*, on which I should like to strum out the modest theme-song of this volume, is austerely defined as 'not having its axis centrally placed', which, even when you restrict it to the narrow field of cricket, seems a rather unimaginative description of a group which embraces, say, the fourth Duke of Richmond, Billy Buttress, Lord Frederick Beauclerk and Mr. Bomber Wells. Roget, on the other hand, goes exuberantly to town with a gallimaufry of sixty-nine synonyms, starting with 'anomalistic' and working up to such 'deranged epitaphs' as 'heteroclite' and 'androgynous'. It may be that if I were to describe one of the professional cricketers of my acquaintance to his face as 'heteroclite' or 'androgynous', he might return fire with alternative adjectives which sounded just as derogatory but much less obscure. Or perhaps not. Cricketers are, on the whole, a kindly and courteous race.

By an eccentric cricketer I mean one who, whether he has lived in the eighteenth or the present less vivid century, whether he has played at 'little' Hambledon or mighty Lord's, has shown to the world some quality of character and individuality which makes him stand out of the ruck; a man around whom legends sprout and grow as thickly as briar roses; a man whose very name raises in the right company a smile of appreciative recollection.

9

I will give you a simple example. Go into any pub in the
West Riding of Yorkshire and mention with such casualness as
you can muster the venerable names, say, of Emmott Robinson
or Arthur Wood. Once you have established your respectful
interest in the masters, your evening will have been made. I
see you departing at closing time, the richer by a wealth of
biographical lore which, if you are the right sort of listener,
will send you home with a warmer heart. Like a good deal of
modern biography, what you hear will contain a fictional
element. The narrative, at any rate, will be delivered with the
utmost solemnity.

So Emmott dreams he dies (the narrator proceeds) and goes
to heaven, see? And the first person he meets at the pearly gate
is Saint Peter.

'How do, Emmott,' he says.

'How do,' says Emmott.

'Now tell me, Emmott,' he says, 'is there anything in your
past life that you're sorry for?'

'Ah, well,' he says, 'maybe I was a bit fond of beer and baccy.'

'Think nowt of it,' says Saint Peter.

'And maybe I was a bit fond of t'lasses, too.'

'Aren't we all?' says Saint Peter.

'And maybe I let slip a bit of language now and then.'

'Tut, tut,' says Saint Peter, 'these things are neither here
nor there. The real question is: have you ever done anything
you've truly regretted?'

'Well,' says Emmott, 'maybe there was one thing. We were
playing Lancashire and we'd set 'em 200 to win on t'last day. So
here they were, last man in, 194 for nine. It's the last ball of the
last over and Harry Makepeace swings his bat like a black-
smith's hammer and hits it a colossal clout. Up and up she goes
and there's me on the boundary leaning back and waiting.
Down she comes at last. If I catch her, we've won; if I miss her,
it's a six and *they've* won. Down she comes.'

'Go on,' says Saint Peter.

'Down and down she comes,' says Emmott in a lingering sort
of voice, 'and then, I hardly like to tell you . . .'

'Nay, Emmott,' cries Saint Peter in a voice of thunder, 'don't
tell me you dropped t'flaming thing.'

The narrator pauses with a nice sense of timing, holding up

his glass for silence, lest a premature lapse into laughter should spoil the cream of the story. 'So next time I sees Emmott, I asks him if this tale is true. "Never in this world," says he, "and I'll tell you for why. Harry Makepeace never hit a ball that high in all his life." '

The audience, which will have smiled in sympathetic fashion over the anxieties of Saint Peter, against whom it bears no malice, chuckles happily over the tailpiece of the story. It savours a character like Emmott Robinson, or, for that matter, like Harry Makepeace, with the same pleasure as a *gourmet* savours a rich dish. Emmott Robinson *is* a rich dish.

II

IT is common talk to assert that nowadays the cricket field, like other fields of human endeavour, lacks both character and characters. Some of this talk is mere routine. In every age you will find complaints of the isn't-what-it-was variety. This sort of thing began with Adam grumbling at the horticultural shortcomings of Cain and Abel and will go on till the last syllable of recorded dialogue. Some of it is plainly unfair, but the strong persistence of the criticism to-day suggests what may be charitably called a certain drabness in the present age.

Elizabethans we may be, but very few of us are Drakes and Raleighs. Critics, guided by their own complexes, will variously blame this drabness on commercial television, the Welfare State, leg-theory bowling, tranquillizing drugs, the Wolfenden Report, and a complete lack of the spirit of adventure. Some of these indiscriminate strictures are less than just. In the last two decades many young people have experienced more adventure than will last them a lifetime. The adventure and the desire for no more of it are equally genuine. Many more have been embraced by a social security which they never had before and which they are now loth to lose. In so many walks of life there is little inducement to lash out. Industrialists and trade unionists alike favour a quiet existence and do very little dashing around. If you ask for gay, carefree cricket, a contemporary cricketer might not unreasonably reply: 'Give us a gay, carefree world to play it in.' Moreover, there is always the argument that if you raise the general level of an age to a plateau (blessed word), you are likely in the course of nature to see fewer peaks. But, whichever way you look at it, the outlook seems fairly permanently dull.

Nevertheless, however flat the level of the age, there will always be some, even though fewer than before, who rise above it. Lancashire may never again see a Crossland who kept his sweater on because he had no shirt beneath it; or a Brearley, who pounded to the crease, leaping over pavilion-gates as though they were part of life's hurdle-race; they may not have a Cecil Parkin, who could say to his captain: 'All right, Mr. Douglas, thee bowl 'em in and I'll go on after tea and bowl 'em out.' But to-day they at least have a young bowler who, when asked in the commentator's honeyed tones if he pronounced his name Greenho, Greenhow or Greenhuff, could reply with superb aplomb: 'I'm not rightly bothered.'

Yorkshire may no longer have a Tom Emmett, who went to his first professional engagement in clogs, with a copy of the *Halifax Courier* as his cricket bag; or a George ('Happy Jack') Ulyett, who claimed that Yorkshire played him for his whistling and good behaviour, but that England sent him in first with W.G. to give the Doctor confidence; or an Alonzo Drake, whose loving mother would demand: 'What's our 'Lonzer keep worriting about Lord Hawke giving him a cap for? *I'll* give him a cap any day of t'week.' But Yorkshire's front line can show a fiery Trueman and a wily Wardle, each of them the hero of a hundred anecdotes, all of them racy and a fair proportion of them printable. The thing called character never quite dies, and characters, though they may seem rarer than of yore, are still worth searching for. When we find them, as we *shall* find them, let us grapple them to our souls with hoops of steel.

Let us be reasonable in our demands for this rare commodity. There are degrees in eccentricity, and perhaps this is just as well. I do not ask that a citizen should be as eccentric as that Earl of Bristol who once stood on one foot on the roof of Milan Cathedral, and drove a coach and six up the steps of Saint Peter's, Rome, no doubt believing all the time that this, dammit, was just the sort of thing a normal Englishman might be expected to do. We may look back in wistfulness rather than in anger on the eighteenth century, that glorious morning of the English eccentric, when every day of his life a gentleman did almost exactly as he pleased and, considering that this freedom gave *carte blanche* to original sin, did surprisingly little long-term harm, even to himself. All power corrupts, we are somewhat arbitrarily informed. Yet, wielding immense power, these people were never completely corrupted and individually they were as nearly incorruptible as any members of any class have ever been in any age. They may have loved wine, as did the younger Pitt, or gambled all night, like Charles James Fox, or committed (and built) strange follies, like Horace Walpole. Yet from any one of these families there may also have sprung a courageous statesman, a profound classical scholar, an imaginative scientist, a fantastic landscape gardener, a pioneer agriculturist to whom succeeding generations of town-dwellers have never been sufficiently grateful.

The eighteenth-century squires were not all as simple-hearted as the noble if slightly idealized Sir Roger de Coverley. They were personally immoral by the standards of the nineteenth century, though not necessarily by those of their own or of ours. They were monumentally, but seldom pettily, selfish. They did not personally create the elegance and charm of their century's domestic architecture, its furniture, its china and its silverware; but their wealth, their patronage—their selfishness, if you like—fostered the climate in which beauty flourished. A man may say what he wishes of the architecture of Bath, of the chairs and tables that came from the hands of Chippendale and Hepplewhite, the chinaware of Josiah Wedgwood, but no man can say that they resulted from the deliberations of a select committee. They were created by individual artists and craftsmen, working under inspired patronage, and the influence of such wise patrons has never wholly faded.

III

BECAUSE the eighteenth century was what it was, cricket, like the other arts, had its aristocratic patrons. Without delving too far into the past, we may say that in the earlier years of the eighteenth century cricket took a firm step forward towards the noble game it was to be. It may be said without snobbery that it became a more interesting game than it had ever been when gentlemen took it up; the game was good for them, and they were good for the game. One man, it can be reasonably argued, cannot play cricket alone. If he handled the bat, he had got to play with others who would bowl and fetch the ball, rank or no rank about them. To join with ordinary people for the sake of a game was the beginning of sportsmanship.

In 1725 the second Duke of Richmond, grandson of Charles II extramaritally (as we now call it), raised an eleven from among the workers on his estate at Goodwood and challenged Sir William Gage, Member of Parliament for Seaford, to bring along his own team and try conclusions. No score of this game has come down to us, but we know that these two captains were 'the joyous pioneers of cricket in Sussex'. Thus we may think of these earliest matches as they were played, neither at Lord's nor on a village green, but in a nobleman's park, shaded by ancient oaks of some great estate. In a picture which shows the game a few years later you can see the wicket, with its two low and slender stumps, surmounted by a single bail, the curved bats, not unlike shortened shinty-sticks; the wicket-keeper, crouching on one knee, his wig discarded in his eagerness; and the scorer, notching away with knife and stick, as he sits, regardless of his doom, in a position perilously near silly-point. It is an endearing picture. The bowling is underhand but markedly purposeful and the players are probably house-servants, grooms, gamekeepers (notoriously men of good eye) and farm-workers on the estate. These were the first professionals and their honourable successors are the young men we admire to-day.

The Duke of Richmond himself was not only one of the first non-playing captains; he may also stand as one of cricket's first great law-makers. It was characteristic of the Duke, and indeed of a general English attitude, that the laws for which he was responsible were not launched on to the world in the abstract, but comprised specific Articles of Agreement, drawn up between his Grace and a Mr. Brodrick, of Surrey, with the purpose of regulating what should happen in a particular game. Here were the beginnings of cricket's laws, and when the Duke gave up cricket and went into the more debatable game of politics, the foundation stone that he had laid remained for the benefit of future cricketers.

It was another Duke who attempted to introduce cricket into France at an unfortunate time. The Duke of Dorset, who was Britain's ambassador in Paris in the seventeen-eighties, deputed William Yalden, of Chertsey, to raise an eleven and bring it over to show 'the art' to the ignorant French in Paris. The team assembled and journeyed by coach to Dover, where they were to take ship for Calais. Dramatically, the Duke, who had come over for a consultation with his government, met them on the quay at Dover and turned them back. The year was 1789, revolution had begun and Paris was no place for John Bullish cricketers. It is a sad story. History is what it is, for good or ill, but it is difficult not to toy with an imaginary score-sheet:

Robespierre b Lumpy 0

Yes, a sad story . . .

Edwin Stead, of Stead Hall, a Kentish landowner, was the father, long before Alfred Mynn and even Lord Harris, of Kent cricket, and in every place where a squire encouraged the game there sprang up on his estate an eager band of grooms and gamekeepers who needed only a word to bring out the cricket that was in them. Afterwards when the Duke of Richmond had passed first into Parliament and then into Paradise, the Sackvilles of Knole became cricket's most distinguished patrons, both in Kent and in the wider fields of England.

In the famous Love Match—that is, the historic match played on the Artillery Ground at Finsbury in 1744 and celebrated by James Love in comparatively immortal verse—the captain of the Kent eleven was Lord John Sackville, who at the critical moment took the catch which decided the result. If any pleasure (or social advancement) was to be obtained by being dismissed by the son of a duke, the batsman enjoyed that satisfaction. Perhaps Lord John showed eccentricity in being a genuine player of the game as well as its patron. Nevertheless, as an aristocratic performer, he takes his place somewhere near the head of an imposing procession of peers which contains the Earl of Winchilsea, who would go anywhere for a game of cricket, the Earl of Tankerville, who (solemn, Wodehouse-ian thought) brought cricket and his butler together, Lord Cornwallis, Lord Darnley, Lord Harris, Lord Hawke, Lord

Willingdon, Lord Jellicoe, Lord Tennyson (Lionel, not Alfred), Lord Aberdare and Lord Cobham.

It is an error to suppose that his Royal Highness the present Duke of Edinburgh is the Royal Family's only cricketer. The Duke of Windsor, wearing a straw hat, was once photographed alongside W. G. Grace, and King Edward VII, when Prince of Wales, once appeared, though with a minimum of success, in a game at Lord's. In the year of the Great Exhibition King Edward's father, the Prince Consort, prevented the Oval from being leased as a building site, thereby, if for no other reason, earning for ever the title of Albert the Good. The first royal cricketer who was both patron and player was Frederick, Prince of Wales, the unlucky son of George II and even unluckier father of George III.

Frederick is one of the minor might-have-beens of history. We know little to his discredit except from those whose professional policy it was to mock and belittle him. Most of the ridicule cast upon him came from his enemy, Hervey, whom Pope denounced as a 'painted child of dirt that stinks and stings'. Frederick and his father did not get on well together, but what Hanoverian father and son ever did? He lived a short life and by no means a gay one. When he died, at a sadly early age, his father incredibly sneered: 'I have lost my eldest son, but I am glad.' During his brief lifetime, he was continually trying to get more money out of his father and/or Parliament. But this desire for more money than they could get was an occupational disease with members of the House of Hanover. It had occurred before Frederick and it occurred after. There lay between Frederick and his father that ill-feeling which a historian of the period has called 'the incurable bane of royalty'. No one has ever stated a reason for the father's ill-will. I believe it was the motiveless malignity of an Iago, all the more evil for being baseless. As did all Princes of Wales of that house, Frederick, for self-protection, was forced to throw in his lot with the parliamentary opposition. The government was strong and the opposition was weak. Walpole, the Prime Minister, bent on a policy which he knew to be cynical but believed to be effective, was a hard man to oppose. In all his political dealings, Frederick had the dirty end of the stick, mainly because his enemies, the sycophantic hangers-on of the Court, were more malevolent and more unscrupulous than he was. The worst that even they could genuinely urge against him was that he was not very bright. And when he died they jeered:

> 'Since it's poor Fred
> There's no more to be said.'

But there is a good deal more to be said. There were many unhappy things in his life. He was twice prevented by his father from marrying the lady he loved. He was also thwarted in his attempt to follow a career in the Army. He had qualities of heart and mind that were rare in his race in that century. Admittedly an eccentric who dressed extravagantly and sometimes behaved unaccountably (though never viciously), he had a love of music, pictures and books, and was happy playing cricket or tennis. It was simply wrong to describe him as 'this ungifted creature'.

Consider what might have happened, had he not been prevented by his father from taking command of the English Army at the time of the Forty-five rising. We cannot tell, but there is no law against wondering. If it had been kindly Fred, instead of his younger brother, Butcher Cumberland, who had led the winning army at Culloden, it is certain that a thousand cruelties and a million black memories might have been avoided. Fred was a cricketer, and no cricketer, whatever his faults, was ever that kind of a butcher. It is a strange irony that he died from a blow struck by a cricket ball. If this fate had happened to his son who became George III, it is arguable that the world might have been saved an infinite deal of trouble.

But let us not pretend that there is anything sacrosanct in the mere fact of being a cricketer. Whether peer or peasant, gentle or simple, cricketers have always been made of the same clay as other men. They have had their successes and failures on and off the field. Many have been clergymen of the Established Church and some, like C. T. Studd, have been Christian missionaries, moved by a spirit of apostolic fire; some have been no better than they should be, and two were hanged for murder. Some have died young, like Fred Grace, in the fullness of their powers, and the tale of those, from K. L.

Hutchings to Hedley Verity, who gave their lives in two world wars, is a story of youthful gallantry that leaves those who hear it with a profound sense of loss. Some, overwhelmed by business anxieties or by ill-health that foreshadowed a total loss of their proud skills, have taken their own lives. Some, like 'Silver Billy' Beldham, the pride of Hambledon's autumnal days, have lived to a great age, looking back over a long succession of golden years.

But, linking them all, as devotees of this game of infinite variety, has been that rich bond of character and comedy which cricket calls forth. Right from Hambledon to whatever is the current season, character and 'characters' live on: 'Lumpy' Stevens, who could dance a jig while drinking his glass of ale; 'mad' Charlie Brown, the Nottingham dyer, who grew so excited when talking of cricket that he splashed his dye into all the neighbouring tubs; Warwick Armstrong, the massive Australian, who during a dull Test read a newspaper in the long field 'to see if he could find any cricket going on anywhere'. There were all these, and hundreds—literally hundreds—more. And against this backcloth of the eccentric and the mildly (or even wildly) abnormal, you have the pattern of the serenely and magnificently normal, as exemplified in such a courteous, even-tempered, untemperamental artist as the professional cricketer who became Sir Jack Hobbs. Here's richness, as Mr. Squeers said; here's richness indeed.

CHAPTER 2

The Wandering Elevens

I

THERE is something almost unbearably nostalgic in the picture of the Wandering Elevens, driving through the leafy lanes of England's green and pleasant land on a summer morning at mid-century. Those peaceful days of the eighteen-fifties and sixties seem to us as far off from us as the beginning of time. Who were the Wandering Elevens? They were the All England Eleven and their rivals and successors, the United England Eleven, teams composed of the cream of English professionals, long before the county championship became the steel framework of English cricket. These elevens were the apostles and missionaries of the game and they had a more enjoyable time of it than missionaries usually have. Richard Daft, that splendid Nottinghamshire batsman, almost dropped into poetry when he described their games.

'What fun we have had in these matches to be sure!' he exclaimed. 'Arrived early, breakfasted on bread, cheese and bottled ale. Tom Foster would leave his umpire's post and come into the pavilion for *more* at the fall of each wicket. . . .' I cannot think of any juster tribute to such noble bread, cheese and bottled ale.

The All England Eleven, as all cricketers know, was founded by its first captain, secretary and manager, that craggy, sardonic old warrior, William Clarke. Under his imperious leadership, the Eleven travelled the length and breadth of rural (and often urban) England, spreading the light of true cricket to the farthest corners of the land. By coach or brake or the uncomfortable train of those early days they travelled, often all through the night, arriving in time for breakfast. But cramped and stiff as they might feel on arrival, they were almost invariably too strong for the local Eighteens or Twenty-twos who had been matched against them. For their part, the

19

local lads were eager to seize their chance of making heroic names for themselves against the ferocious bowling of Jackson and Tarrant, just as they might, with equally desperate hardihood, have striven to stand up to the professional bruiser at the local fair. As small boys, W. G. Grace and his elder brother, E.M., played against the All England Eleven, and may be said to have seen their first great cricketers in matches of this kind.

The All England Eleven had its hey-day before the time of Test matches, overseas tours and county cricket as we understand such things to-day. Each player was proud of, and famous in, the county to which he belonged, but in the eighteen-fifties it was more important to play for the All England Eleven than for any county. Old Clarke was a Nottingham man and some of his most powerful clansmen, like the elegant Joseph Guy, the ferocious fast bowler, John Jackson, and George Parr, who succeeded Clarke as captain, were Notts men, too. Kent was represented by those legendary characters, Alfred Mynn and Fuller Pilch, a Norfolk man who had settled in Canterbury. Surrey contributed such distinguished members as Martingell and Tom Sewell, who were fixtures at the Oval even before the famous gasholders. They were a mixed but distinguished lot. Clarke held his men together with a firm and, as some said, parsimonious hand; it was, in fact, his tightness of hand which eventually brought disruption to their company. But before the break-up, and while the Eleven remained united amongst themselves, they were indeed a happy band of pilgrims.

Clarke was so typically the Victorian individualist that it is a little surprising to discover that he was born a couple of years before the end of the eighteenth century. He was originally apprenticed to the bricklaying trade, but was early in showing his talent as a cricketer. At eighteen he began a career with his county and for the next thirty years was its leading character. He was Nottinghamshire's commanding general, just as old Nyren had been Hambledon's eighty years before. All this time his fame, though considerable, was mainly local, and he was nearly forty-eight years old when the M.C.C. asked him to come up to Lord's as a practice bowler. During the seven years that followed, his success as a bowler was staggering: in that time he took well over 2,300 wickets, an average of nearly 350 a season. Even 'Tich' Freeman, that greedy wicket-taker, never gathered quite such a harvest. Clarke's lowest annual bag was 222; his largest, in his last year of the seven, was 476. Let us grant that his team played mainly against local Eighteens and Twenty-twos, that the opposition usually contained a high percentage of rabbits, and that he simply hated taking himself off. In spite of all these things, the figure of 2,385 wickets remains colossal.

His bowling action was as odd as was his general attitude at the crease. He would amble amiably up to the wicket, swing his arm back in a peculiar way, till it was almost level with his armpit, thus shooting the ball out from the highest point at which it could decently retain the name of under-hand. When it landed from this horrid height it was apt to sit straight up, like a dog begging. Delivered with bewildering changes in flight and a deadly spin, it is perhaps no wonder that this ball, with its myriad variations, took 2,385 wickets.

With a character as strong as his bowling was cunning, he was bound to get a good deal of his own way. As captain of the Eleven, Old Clarke could bowl as long as he wished and from the end that suited him best. 'I'll bowl from this end,' he would say; 'you can have which end you like.' He had a wicked eye for the pretentious and his tongue was as sharp as a razor. ('Eye' is correct, for he had but one, having lost the other through an accident at fives.) When asked by a raw youngster what was the first step to becoming a great bowler, he growled, with an old-fashioned sideways glance: 'Get your finger-nails cut.' And when a proud mother boasted of her tall son: 'He's six feet in stockings,' he replied: 'What a lot of toes he must have.' Like many a bowler before or since, he had little charity in his heart for those who deprived him of wickets by dropping catches. One luckless fieldsman who, having dropped a sitter in the first innings, asked where he should go in the second. 'Stand about anywhere you like,' Old Clarke grunted; 'there'll be plenty of balls flying about presently. Maybe you'll be able to hold one of them . . . if you're lucky.'

In the end Clarke married the landlady of the Trent Bridge Inn. It was almost the perfect ending to a Dick Whittington story Or perhaps an Aladdin story? If he could return for a moment to catch a glimpse of the proud Trent Bridge ground,

home of the first Test match in many a season, he might well
think that it could only have been brought there by rubbing a
wonderful lamp.

Clarke's chief lieutenant, George Parr, followed him as captain and gave an added distinction both to the leadership and
to the batting of the Eleven. They called him the Lion of the
North, and this was a tribute not only to the magnificent
leonine head that you may see in his photograph, but to his
power and artistry as a batsman. After the mighty Fuller Pilch
had retired, there was no batsman in England to touch him.
Though Parr succeeded Pilch by natural right at the top of
the tree, he was not an artist of Pilch's classic majesty; perhaps
he was the first of the great 'mobile' players. He played back
with strokes as powerful as those with which Pilch had played
forward. His cutting, both square and late, was a thing not of
beauty, but of dynamic power. Just as you have seen Compton
do, he would daringly move down the pitch to meet the enemy
in a manner almost unknown among his contemporaries and,
again like Compton, he could take the spectator's breath away
with his audacious sweep to leg. A legend has come down
to us that he would pull a straight ball off his off stump over
square-leg's head, and he may well have done this on occasion, but it was really E. M. Grace, who employed this unorthodox stroke as a matter of punitive policy. Parr's leg-hitting,
nevertheless, was colossal. Near the square-leg boundary, that is,
if you are right-handed and batting at the pavilion end, there is
an old elm stump, which is all that remains of 'George Parr's
tree', so called because so many of his mighty leg-hits found
their way into its branches.

Richard Daft, who became the Eleven's captain after George
Parr's retirement, has left a series of unforgettable little pictures of the great man. George was the son of a gentleman
farmer of Radcliffe-on-Trent, and was born in a fine ivy-
mantled old manor. William Clarke, who always knew a good
man when he saw one, brought him out into good cricket when
he was eighteen. After this introduction he remained in cricket
of the highest class until the end of his honourable career. He
was, Daft says, of an oddly nervous temperament, for, though
the bowling of bumpers did not bother him in the least, he
was scared of thunderstorms and, from the first moment he

boarded a ship, believed himself marked for drowning as
surely as Jonah. On every journey he reverently carried a
battered leather hat-box, the contents of which were (and for
ever remained) a mystery. It seemed to be, not to speak profanely, a sort of Ark of the Covenant. He would glare at any
officious hotel or railway porter who offered to relieve him of
it. It even became an offence for anyone to look in its direction
after the Eleven had lost a match. Nearly twenty years after his
retirement, Parr was persuaded to travel as far as Yorkshire
with the All England Eleven to stand as umpire and, sure
enough, he arrived at the station carrying, as if he had never
put it down, the same old hat-box with the same old dint in its
side. What was more, he expressed surprise that his younger
friend should have recognized the sacred object.

'Recognize it?' cried Daft. 'Why, I'd recognize it if I met it
fifty years hence in the jungles of Central Africa.'

Parr captained the side that was the first of all the touring
teams in the adventurous voyage to America in 1859, and was
the team's best batsman if its worst sailor. When he died in
1891 they buried him in the churchyard of his native village
and among the many wreaths that covered his coffin was one
made from a branch of 'Parr's tree'. No man could have received a nobler epitaph than Richard Daft's tribute to his old
chief, 'the Lion of the North, for years the mainstay of his
county, and of the Players of England, the captain of the
famous All England Eleven, and the finest batsman in the
world; a man under whose banner I am proud to have fought,
for a more honest and straightforward cricketer never took
hold of a bat'.

II

OUR most vivid accounts of the All England Eleven come not
from its semi-mythical days of Alfred Mynn, Fuller Pilch and
the schoolmaster-artist who called himself 'Felix'. These were
almost legendary days, though their scores are accurately set
down in their appointed place. Richard Daft's entrancing
narrative covers the period ten to fifteen years later when
George Parr was skipper, when Hayward, of Cambridgeshire,
and Richard Daft himself were the leading batsmen and the
most terrifying bowlers were John (Foghorn) Jackson and

George (Tear 'em) Tarrant. These two bowlers probably did
more to encourage a spirit of adventure among local cricketers
than anyone else of their generation. To face Jackson and
Tarrant you simply *had* to have courage if nothing else.

The next most famous character was Julius Cæsar, the most
dapper member of the Eleven, who came, not from Rome, but
from Godalming, and whose batting was as neat as his person
was natty. He seems to have insisted on having his full name—
Julius, never J.—set down in the scorebook. He could always
be relied on to make runs by handsome strokes and, on tour,
he carried a monster portmanteau, which was as much his
mysterious but faithful companion as was George Parr's
hallowed hat-box. The portmanteau was so big that it can never
have been anything like full and Cæsar's more humorous companions—if the crime must be laid at one door, I suspect John
Jackson—took a fiendish pleasure in slapping down the
heaviest luggage on top of it, so that it was squashed almost
flat and practically disappeared beneath the strain.

Cæsar was by temperament a mild little man who sometimes
got himself into unwanted quarrels, notably on the famous
tour of '59 with George Parr's team in America. A fine boxer,
he had the good boxer's admirable quality of self-control; indeed, he was so peaceful in intent that he was more than
polite to every American he met in the course of his travels and
praised everything American at England's expense. There is,
however, a limit to pacifism, however far back the pacifist may
lean. One evening he found himself in conversation with an
American in a New York saloon, where 'London porter' was
being served. The porter was warming and heartening. Indeed, it was more, for almost imperceptibly, to change the
metaphor, it touched off the spring of Julius Cæsar's long-
repressed patriotism. To his own surprise, he heard himself
offering in the most bellicose manner to punch that gentleman's nose. What was even more alarming than any other
reason was that the other fellow suddenly whipped out a six-
shooter and poked it into Julius's face. What should Mr. J.
do? Like a true man of peace he laughed heartily, as though
this were the best joke in the world. Then with friendly
words and humorously placatory gestures, he backed slowly
towards the swing doors, an action you have often seen per-

formed by the comedy character in a Western film. The instant he reached the doorway, he turned and ran like a hare towards his own hotel, expecting at every stride he took a bullet to bowl him between his off and leg shoulder-blades. Next morning he made known his solemn resolve: 'The first Yank I meet on English soil, I'll give him a hiding, if I get three months for it.'

But no hiding was ever administered. Cæsar recovered his equanimity. The American nation was forgiven.

There is now a law against what is, I think, called persistent intimidation by fast bowling at the batsman's person. The final decision is left to the umpire's discretion, but it is obvious that the bowler's attitude, to attract rebuke, must be one of constructive malice. I do not know exactly what happens. I assume that, after a bumper or two, the umpire says: 'Steady, Fred'; the bowler says 'Sorry, George', and then peace reigns. A hundred years ago a fast bowler did not have to be naughty. The pitches of the period saw to it that he was intimidating merely because he was fast. 'Jackson's pace is very fearful,' says the elegy on Alfred Mynn, which is incidentally the second-best cricket poem in the language. No doubt Jackson's pace was all that, and it was made even more fearful by the fact that, the moment he had taken a wicket, he blew his nose with a sound like thunder. That is how his nickname of Foghorn was born. He was, to use the phrase oftenest applied to him, a rough-and-tumble fellow, and was continually in and out of scrapes, as you might expect that kind of fast bowler to be. John Jackson, Suffolk-born and with more than a touch of gypsy blood in him, was a big, powerful man and the hurricane speed of his round-arm bowling was apt to render his opponents of the Eighteens and Twenty-twos what a later character was to describe as 'a trifle apprehensive'. A 'hover' from Jackson, as *Punch* described it, was as near a nightmare as human mind could imagine. His figures against the Eighteens comprised not so much a bowling analysis as a record of slaughter. On the other hand, he was never pleased at being hit, and when the ebullient 'Buns' Thornton twice drove him out of the field off successive balls, he growled: 'Oh, to hell with that kind o' batting!'

The most fascinating picture of Foghorn Jackson is por-

trayed in Daft's description of the Eleven's tour in Cornwall.
After a coach drive over a road so rough that it almost scared
the nervous George Parr out of his wits, not to mention a
fellow-travelling Crimean veteran, who soothed his own
terrors by an unending stream of profanity, the cricketers
knocked up the owner of a lonely farm, who was as deaf as an
adder. Misunderstanding their intentions, he attempted to
drive them off with a blunderbuss, but afterwards accepted
their bellowed explanations, relented and gave them bread
and cheese. John Jackson suddenly disappeared and later
emerged from the dairy, looking as though he had been inter-
rupted in the midst of a well-lathered shave. He had merely
been burying his face, with the best of intentions, in a great
bowl of clotted cream. And that was the last of the cream that
his comrades ever saw.

Very few cricketers before W.G. ever attained the honour
of a personal appearance in *Punch*. Jackson did. Imagine the
dialogue appended to the picture of a gentleman returning
from the wicket, muffled from top to toe in bandages, as from
the wars.

'Good match, old fellow?'

'Oh yes; awfully jolly.'

'What did you do?'

'I had a hover of Jackson; first ball 'it me on the 'and; the
second 'ad me on the knee; the third was in my eye; and the
fourth bowled me out!'

If you were terrified of Jackson at one end, you would find
naught for your comfort at the other. You could only feel as
the Australians of 1954–55 must have felt when they escaped
from the speed of Statham, only to fall into the terrors of
Tyson.

George (Tear 'em) Tarrant, of the once-famous shire of
Cambridge, though not so massively hostile in appearance,
was almost as fearful in pace as Jackson himself. His run up to
the wicket, like Tyson's, was of immense length. He became,
whether he knew it or not, the mentor of the mightier
Spofforth, for when he visited Australia with George Parr's
team in 1863–64, the Demon, as a young imp, watched him
from the Melbourne boundary, and swore that when he grew
up he would bowl even faster. Tarrant was not a six-footer, like

Jackson, but he tore up to the wicket with a fury that lost nothing from his shortage of inches. He had a few seasons of outstanding success, bowling devastatingly both for his county and the Players. Unhappily, he died young. In his short life-time he was not, we are told, a lovable character, but must a fast bowler be lovable? The moralists, I think, ask too much of him. His business is to attack, with passionate fervour, three straight sticks. Anything that intervenes between him and his target is almost bound to be damaged. Tarrant did not relish being hit, and if you were so lucky or so injudicious as to take a six off him, you put your life in mortal peril. The next few deliveries flew round your ears like misguided missiles. He had the reputation of being evil-tempered, but history records only one instance of this, when at Fenner's in 1861 for Cambridge-shire against Middlesex he shamefully refused to go in, because Newman was allowed to play when Carpenter was hurt in the field. As, however, he was in fact a first-class boxer, his temper, except when being hit out of the ground, was reasonably con-trolled. He did not, any more than did Julius Cæsar, go about trailing his coat. On long-distance tours among outlandish people, he would act as his captain's bodyguard. When anyone attempted to pick a quarrel with George Parr, he would murmur: 'Go at him, Tear 'em!' Then, but not till then, Tarrant would oblige, which was a sign, I think, of a pretty equable temperament.

Tarrant, for one reason or another, but mainly for one, was addicted to arriving at unscheduled destinations. He once travelled by himself to a match and arrived, in a moment of what we may charitably call aberration, at Horncastle in Lincolnshire instead of Harecastle in Cheshire. When he finally turned up at tea-time on the third day, George Parr observed tartly: 'It's a good job that you got only as far away as Lincolnshire.'

The best judges of the day said: 'When you have Jackson, Tarrant and Freeman, you have the best three bowlers in Eng-land.' That was true, but John Lillywhite's observation on the havoc wrought by Jackson and Tarrant was also true. 'After a visit from the crack eleven,' said John, 'the local chemists sold more arnica than all the rest of the year.'

III

THERE came a day when the first glories of the All England
Eleven faded into ill-will. The goodly fellowship became un-
soldered, mainly, perhaps, because Old Clarke had a high hand
and a tight fist. He was, as the cabmen said of Mr. Dickens, a
'harbitrary gent' and he was far too eloquent in what we should
now call 'tearing off a strip'. Some of the players whom he had,
over a long period, rubbed the wrong way, determined to start
an eleven of their own. The leaders of the schism were Jemmy
Dean and Johnny Wisden, who convened a meeting at the
Adelphi Hotel, Sheffield, on 6th September, 1852, and prevailed upon every member of their colleagues to sign a kind of
grand remonstrance, stating that they would not take part in
any match (county matches excepted) of which Clarke had
management or control 'in consequence of the treatment they
had received from him at Newmarket and elsewhere'. Now,
what happened at Newmarket remains a deep mystery, like
the famous story of the Grouse and the Gunroom, but it is
probable that some arbitrary word or deed, uttered or committed by the old tyrant at Newmarket, did duty as the last
straw. The previous load of straw was no doubt the smallness
of the wages paid by Clarke, for even the best of his players
received no more than £4 to £6 a week, out of which he had to
pay all his expenses.

As is the way of splinter parties, the new men affirmed their
solidarity by calling themselves the United England Eleven
and soon there were two eminent teams following their missionary and educational journeys. What is more, there were
enough fine cricketers to furnish two splendid elevens and
there was enough interest in the game even in the remotest
districts to keep those two elevens successfully touring for the
best part of the next twenty years.

Besides Dean and Wisden, the most eminent seceder was
Jemmy Grundy, and heroes who joined the new eleven a little
later were Bob Carpenter, of Cambridgeshire, and William
Caffyn, of Surrey, who went to Australia with a touring side
and remained to coach the spiritual ancestors of Miller and
Lindwall.

It was difficult to establish good relations during William Clarke's lifetime, but when he died in 1856, old animosities softened and the great gulf fixed between the two Elevens was bridged. They met at Lord's on 1st June, 1857, before a crowd of 10,000, the biggest 'gate' that a cricket match had ever drawn till then. The All England Eleven, after a fierce battle, won by five wickets and for nearly a dozen years, that is, until W.G.'s domination set the Gentlemen *v.* Players series in the lead, the game, All England Eleven *v.* United England Eleven, was the match of the season.

When the two Elevens met head-on, these were homeric encounters. There was one pitched battle when they faced each other at Lord's in 1860; it was fought out, inch by inch, and in the end the All England Eleven won a low-scoring game by 21 runs, mainly through a stalwart second innings of 55, worth many a century, by George Parr, and positively sadistic fast bowling by Tarrant and Jackson.

When the sides met again at Lord's the following year, for the benefit of the Cricketers' Fund, the game was even more palpitating. Jackson once more bowled diabolically and, by a fiercely hit 41 at No. 10, just turned the scale to give the All Englanders the victory by 5 runs, despite an heroic rearguard action by George Griffith, of Surrey.

Jemmy Grundy, of Notts, was a teasing medium-pace bowler who was hard to play and still harder to score off. If the pitch broke up or he 'found a spot', he was more devastating than even Jackson or Tarrant. On the field he wore a black velvet cap which he purposefully pushed into his belt when he went on to bowl. Off the field he had a passion for fat mutton chops. The United Eleven's most consistent batsman was Bob Carpenter, whose county companion, Hayward, was one of two or three leading bats on the other side. The two are often photographed together, the finest opening pair of their period (with the finest pairs of whiskers), the Hobbs and Sutcliffe of their time. You will remember from old photographs their slightly sawn-off bowler hats, rather in the George Robey manner, and their white shirts adorned with red spots. They were even better together than separate. Nobody asks whether Hobbs was better than Sutcliffe. Hobbs, not to dispute an indisputable fact, was better than anybody, but Hobbs, with Sutcliffe at the other end, was even greater than his great self. There was something similar in the partnership of Hayward and Carpenter. Hayward was slim and straight, elegant in form as in style. He held his bat by the end of the handle, scored swiftly all round the wicket in the classic 'forward' manner, and never made a stroke that was not a joy to look upon. Carpenter was more solid in defence and displayed a whole armoury of powerful back strokes with which he would punish the slow bowlers.

The name Wisden is, after Grace, perhaps the most famous in cricket, if for a rather different reason. His renown rests on his reputation as cricket's immortal chronicler, but his talents on the field were considerable. He was one of the best all-rounders of that middle period; a dynamic little man, who stood five feet four inches in height and weighed in his playing days no more than seven stone. In one season he out-Clarked Clarke by taking 455 wickets, bowling in a style described as 'very straight, accurate in length, very fast and ripping'. He had a swift bowling action and a habit of swinging his bat so that it looked like the pendulum of a grandfather clock. Writing of his beloved game, he gave his picture of the happy cricketer:

'To be a good cricketer is to be wary yet bold; self-possessed yet cautious; strong yet gentle; firm yet manly.'

The famous *Cricketers' Almanack* was not the first of cricket's annual records (this was Lillywhite's *Guide to Cricketers*, which first appeared in 1845). But Wisden's is the one that has lasted and its first number, published at a shilling, comprised a first trickle of that river of information and statistics which has since swelled out into an ocean. Some of the *Almanack's* accounts of early matches were written in prose that had a classic ring. Reporting the conclusion of the 1870 Gentlemen *v.* Players match, Wisden said:

'No hands clapped, no voice cheered him as Southerton, the last man in, walked to the wickets; so quiet, so strangely quiet, at that moment were the spectators, who, however, cheered wildly when Price, at the other end, by a cut for 2 made it 8 to win, and louder still when a leg-bye, and a single by each batsman, brought it five to win; but there the match finished. . . .'

So the two elevens pursued their separate ways throughout the length and breadth of the land until late in the sixties.

They were, like everything else that is human, the victims of change, but one thing is certain: their travels and their prowess provided cricket's finest spectacle until the county championship proper gave rivalry a local habitation and a name.

CHAPTER 3

Doctor at the Crease

I

Who was cricket's most famous doctor? There is no prize for the answer, because the question is too easy. There have been enough cricketing doctors to run a health service; to glance at only a few: W.G.'s friend, W. G. Heasman of Sussex; E. M. Ashcroft of Derbyshire; J. J. Cameron of the West Indies; R. L. Park of Victoria; L. O. S. Poidevin, the Lancashire Australian; Sir H. W. Russell Bencraft of Hampshire; H. V. Horden of New South Wales, whom Sir Jack Hobbs thought the most troublesome of googly bowlers; and H. C. Pretty, who scored a century in his first county game (for Surrey) and later, for Northamptonshire, hit a 200 in as many minutes in days when the whole side topped the two hundred seldom enough. W.G. himself had four brothers, and all of them doctors, except (strictly speaking) for poor Fred, whom the gods must have loved, for he died a little short of his finals and his thirtieth birthday.

There was Henry, born in 1833—'he was a good doctor, he was,' said W.G.; there was Alfred, born in 1840, the boxer of the family and the only one who smoked; and there was Edward Mills, born in 1841, who would have made the name of Grace famous, even if—profane supposition—W.G. had never existed.

It is impossible to give W.G. more than his due. It is easy to give E.M. less. He began cricket almost as soon as he could hold a bat and he never gave up as long as there was breath in his sturdy body. The historic letter which Mrs. Grace wrote to William Clarke regarding the potential prowess of her sons is usually quoted as the first stepping-stone in W.G.'s career, but, while admitting its insistence that the younger lad's defence was stronger, we must remember that it was in fact written to recommend E.M. to the captain of the All England Eleven.

32

E.M. actually played against the visiting All England Eleven at the age of thirteen, while W.G., *ætate* six, sat with his mother in the family pony chaise and watched. In this match E.M. was given l.b.w. to a ball that hit his diminutive front elevation in the chest, but he fielded with agility at long-stop, a key position in those days, and gained golden opinions from Old Clarke himself.

Those summer mornings when the Grace family played on their own pitch in the orchard at Downend saw some of the most truly enchanted hours in cricket's chequered story; with the dew of the morning upon them, they come as brightly to the memory as a scene in a Shakespearian comedy: the shouts of the boys; the frenzied barking of the three canine fieldsmen, Don, Ponto and Noble; the Polonian advice of Uncle Pocock: 'Play straight, boy, play straight.' W.G. obeyed the counsel of perfection and played straight. E.M. reversed the poet's advice to 'scorn delights and live laborious days'. He scorned the laborious duty of the straight bat and revelled in unorthodox delights, pulling savagely at straight or off balls. This brought disapproving growls from Ponto, who had to burst through the orchard hedge, follow each hit and retrieve it from the wood beyond the stream.

E.M., young though he was, had worked mightily hard with his father and elder brother Henry preparing the orchard pitch, which had involved the cutting down of several apple trees. When the wicket had been cut and rolled, he joined in the bowling team, which included Henry and Uncle Pocock, and that is how W.G. received his first batting practice.

E.M.'s entry into spheres higher than club cricket was less of an entry than an assault. At the age of twenty he played (as a substitute) for an M.C.C. side against Kent at Canterbury and caused what was virtually the greatest sensation in the cathedral city since the murder of Thomas à Becket. His score was 196 and in Kent's second innings he took all ten wickets. When he went out to Australia with George Parr's team in 1863, he was, says *Wisden*, 'the biggest run-getter in the world', and he held that position until he came home and found that he had a younger brother capable of surpassing him. But only W.G. could have done it. W.G. rose to great heights by playing orthodox strokes harder and straighter than anybody else had ever played them. E.M. rose in blatant defiance of the orthodox.

Like 'Monkey' Hornby, and, for that matter, like Napoleon Bonaparte, E.M. made up for his lack of inches by a devouring energy and by some incandescent internal force. He wanted to hit a six (all run for preference) off every ball he received; he wanted to get a wicket, by force or cunning, with every ball he bowled; and if he was neither batting nor bowling, he *willed* the batsman to send him a catch, the harder the better, in one of the suicidal positions. An old Gloucestershire cricketer once told me: 'Where did E.M. field? He'd start a yard from the bat at point *and then creep in.*'

His batting was a one-man blitz. Every ball, he seemed to argue, ought to be hit and every hit ought to be run out to the maximum; his method of running 'impossible' runs could demoralize the field and occasionally his partners, though, to be quite fair, nobody could ever rattle W.G. When E.M. and W.G. went in first together for Gloucestershire or for the Gentlemen—they opened only once for England—they liked to play tip and run, the striker darting to mid-off, in a manner which in time drove frenzied fieldsmen to shy the ball practically anywhere but near the stumps. That perfection of timing and scientific precision in run-stealing achieved later by Hobbs and Rhodes, and later still by Hobbs and Sutcliffe, was as different from the run-robbery of E.M. and W.G. as the humane-killer from the pole-axe. Both were deadly, but the pole-axe caused the victim more distress. It was not until the brethren had been separated in any particular innings that the ravaged fieldsmen became even convalescent.

E.M.'s tremendous pull, which was to break more hearts than honest Ponto's, was more daring and more characteristic than any other batsman's, *not* even excepting Patsy Hendren's, but it was far from being his only stroke. He had several others, of which the most alarming was an off-drive which sent the ball skimming like a rifle bullet past or over mid-off. Its trajectory rose swiftly, but never very steeply, and sailed for six nicely clear of long-off's upstretched hands. With these two shots, and several even less orthodox ones, he exasperated the family dogs and two generations of English and Australian fieldsmen.

No bowler could bowl E.M. a ball with any certainty of what would eventually happen to it. Straight or widish balls on the

off might well be dispatched straight over square-leg, while a
yorker on the leg stump might pass, still soaring, over long-off's
head, and the poor bowler had to cope with every form of
violence in between. E.M.'s footwork, if not so dainty, was as
effective as Nijinsky's. His older brother Alfred once humorously asserted that no bowler could bowl a ball bad enough to
get E.M. out. He never failed to deal discouragingly with the
good ones.

In his early years he was a round-arm bowler of some speed,
but while he was in Australia with George Parr's team in 1863–
64 he hurt his arm. It was characteristic of the man that this
accident should have occurred while he was in the act of throwing the cricket ball 120 yards against an aboriginal. The
damage to the arm was further aggravated by a hunting accident
the following winter. As a result, he turned himself into a slow
and cunning lob bowler, with quite a monstrous bag of wickets
to show every season. As a fieldsman, he never threw in over-
arm again, but developed a method of jerking in with great
speed and accuracy from the most distant parts of the field.
As he grew older he took an increasingly wicked pleasure in
fielding closer to the bat. Once A. N. Hornby, Lancashire's
captain and an equally determined individualist, observed
dispassionately: 'If you stay there, E.M., I'll kill you.'

'Kill away, Monkey,' retorted E.M.

The very next ball received a murderous slash. There was
a resounding smack as though a brick, ferociously propelled,
had hit an oak fence. Then the ball flew high in the air, whither
E.M. had exultantly flung it. Hornby paused for a moment,
incredulous, and then stumped away, glaring. In this manner
E.M. once caught A. E. Stoddart, a batsman of speed and violence, so close to the bat that he was able to hand the ball to
the wicket-keeper without budging a step.

In 1896 E.M. retired from regular appearance in county
games, though he remained Gloucestershire's eccentric but
efficient secretary for another dozen years. As captain of his
club at Thornbury, he went on almost endlessly, voraciously
seeking runs and wickets as a lion seeks its prey. In his palmy
days of 1875, in one kind of cricket or another (and most of it
pretty good), he took 369 wickets in the season.

The immense length of his playing life did not change his

temperament. As a youngster he had batted with supreme confidence against the fastest and best, Jackson, Tarrant, Willsher
and other terrors. In mid-career he played against (and dealt
faithfully with) such giants as Palmer, Ferris and Spofforth.
In the first Test match ever played in England (in 1880) he
opened the English innings with W.G. in a highly satisfactory
partnership of just under a hundred. The same year he played
his finest game against the Australians. His scores were only
65 and 41, and Gloucestershire failed to win the match, but
Spofforth's dark brows grew darker as E.M., to the spectators'
ecstatic astonishment, hooked him to the square-leg boundary
again and again. In his later years for Gloucestershire E.M. met
Lohmann, Richardson, J. T. Hearne and the other county
bowlers of that fruitful period and there was none that inspired
terror in him.

At the turn of the century E.M. sent to the editor of *Wisden*
an account of his figures in all kinds of matches, beginning with
his first match in 1851, when he was ten years old, and ending
forty-eight years later. He made no comment on these gargan-
tuan statistics, except to report that in the year 1885 he had had
a bad knee and could not play. In the forty-nine years, he cal-
culated that he had taken 10,006 wickets and scored over 72,000
runs. Wait a moment longer.

I do not know his figures for the intervening years, but in
1905 he was complaining with asperity that (once more because
of the bad knee) he had hardly captured 200 wickets by the
first week in July. By an extra effort he rallied his strength and
finished this poor season with a bag of 303. In 1906 he seemed
to have recovered completely, for his toll of wickets rose at the
end of that season to 352. Whatever we may think, this was not
bad for a working doctor of sixty-five. In 1909, his very last
season, he took 119 wickets. There is no word for those fifty-
nine years but Dominie Sampson's: prodigious.

The story of the Thornbury club, under his paternalistic
leadership, is a saga in itself. As Thornbury's chief bowler, he
first mesmerized, then pulverized the enemy; as Thornbury's
leading batsman, he hit the foe out of sight. It is recorded that
the village post-master, who faithfully officiated as the home
umpire, would always take up his stand at the wicket with the
pockets of his white coat bulging with cricket balls. This was to

ensure that, whenever E.M. hit a ball into the roadway, the next one could be presented to him for the purpose of hitting another six with as little delay as possible. The maximum number carried by the post-master was nine and, in the course of one enormous first-wicket stand, E.M. finished off every one of them. I am not sure if his subsequent declaration would be set down in the scorebooks as 200 for none or 200 for nine.

He once arrived on the field for a game against a neighbouring village with but two men in close support instead of the more conventional ten. But nothing could dismay him. His two companions were C. J. Robinson, his partner in many an opening stand for Thornbury, and F. L. Cole, a loyal subordinate and, what was equally important, a capable wicketkeeper. From among the crowd which had gathered to see the fun, E.M. arbitrarily selected (and forthwith conscripted) eight characters, most of whom had never played cricket in their lives and never meant to; E.M., however, held them with his glittering eye and into the game they had to go, as surely as if they had been shanghaied. When E.M. and Robinson, batting first, had made 147, E.M. was unaccountably out. After that the batting was never quite so exuberant, but by the time the innings ended, Cole and the conscripts had raised the total to 156. The only method by which Thornbury could now win the match was for E.M. and Robinson to bowl the enemy out twice. This task they not only undertook with relish, but performed in remarkably quick time. In the course of the two innings, E.M. took fourteen wickets, mostly clean bowled, and thought nothing of it.

There is little doubt that, in a forceful and forthright family, E.M. was the most forceful and forthright. They all, in their various ways, wanted to win and perhaps he demanded victory more urgently than any of them. The brothers could bicker cheerfully among themselves in their solid, clannish way, but when the stronghold of the family (or the county) was threatened, they would close their ranks to stand four-square; and when the Graces performed this solemn military evolution their standard-bearer would be E.M.

In country sports, of which cricket was only one, he would ride harder and shoot straighter than any of them. He was a first-class runner and jumper and, considering their difference in length of limb, he was no easy victim for W.G. in athletic contests. Once in the hunting field his horse leaped over a five-barred gate, leaving E.M. behind. Instantly, almost in the same action, E.M. was seen to scramble to his feet, clear the gate, catch up with his horse and hurl himself into the saddle again. If any man thinks this is an easy feat, let him try it, encumbered by tailcoat, tight breeches and heavy riding-boots.

In contemporary legend E.M. competes with 'Monkey' Hornby as a man of wrath and a harasser of the barracker. Maybe cricketers to-day are more civilized; assuredly, they are less downright. Of all contemporary cricketers, Keith Miller, that magnificent extrovert, is the only one who has ever raised his hand to a barracker, except in the way of kindness. On receipt of insult, E.M. would leave the crease, chase the insulter (or insulters) out of the ground and then come back to finish his innings, unpuffed and with an added jauntiness, due to a sense of justice done to the evil-doer. After the match between Gloucestershire and the 1896 touring side had prematurely ended in the county's virtual annihilation, E.M. challenged the Australian, H. Donnan, to a single-wicket match. As E.M. ran up to bowl, some of the drunks who were seen more frequently at cricket matches then than now began a chorus of jeers. E.M. turned on the ringleader like a charging rhinoceros and the unhappy toper, the fear of death heavily upon him, incontinently fled. Out of the ground and over the Downs the chase proceeded and E.M. was absent for a long time. When he got back, even his most facetious friends felt diffident about asking him what he had done with the body.

'He's still running,' said E.M. grimly, and imagination toys with the fancy that somewhere on Ashley Down on moonlight nights the ghost of E.M.'s injudicious critic, 'with face ghastly white', flees in eternal terror from a sturdy, and less ghostly, pursuer.

Hardly ever, I repeat, has E.M. received his due meed of praise. W.G. is great, and Thomson is his prophet, but it is not to be disputed that E.M. carved out the way for him, blazing the Graces' trail through the mid-century forest. Even W.G. was in those early days hardly E.M.'s equal in sheer daring or in ability to swing a losing game completely round into victory by grabbing the bowling by the scruff of the neck. Without dis-

respect to to-day's cricket, I believe it would have been hard for
modern bowlers, however skilfully negative or negatively skilful they might be, to keep E.M. permanently in subservience.
'Arm me audacity!' was his motto and if human courage and
resource could have any avail, E.M. would have battled his way
out of the most cunning trap.

Of his work as secretary of the Gloucestershire county club
it is impossible to speak without admiration, not to say awe. He
was the first holder of the post when the club was founded,
mainly through his father's efforts, in 1870, and he held it for
thirty-eight years. All that time on the troublesome and
time-taking job, he was a one-man administration, never
grousing and never asking for clerical assistance. After
his playing days were over, he could be seen on the
Bristol ground at the beginning of the season, walking
briskly round among the members and potential members,
joking with one, 'telling off' another, stuffing their sub-
scription money higgledy-piggledy into his pockets, but invariably sending each man his receipt and his ticket by the
same evening's post. He never missed a committee meeting,
and seldom refrained from giving his opinion on matters of
policy. Whether they wanted it or not, the committee got it, and
if they declined to let him vote, he would know the reason why.
On his retirement a testimonial was raised for him throughout
the county and its total came to £600. It was only a token pay-
ment, for service of the kind he gave cannot be rewarded in
money.

When E.M. was twenty years old, Arthur Haygarth wrote
of him as a young man 'overflowing with cricket at every pore,
full of lusty life, cheerily gay, with energy inexhaustible. . . .'
What was said of him at twenty could have been said with equal
force at sixty. As long as there was breath in his body, he was
'full of lusty life'. I cannot imagine a richer combination.

II

I am thinking of another sporting practitioner, a later contemporary of the Graces. His first name, like that of so many good
men, was Arthur and, though he was the sort of all-rounder
who had indulged in pastimes as exuberantly varied as boxing,
football (both codes), golf, billiards, ski-ing, flying in its early

stages, and whaling, cricket was for long his dearest love. Apart from the playful buckling of a couple of ribs at rugger, all his most interesting wounds were inflicted by a cricket ball. Love is a most irrational emotion and Arthur, an Irishman born in Scotland, behaved all through, as you might expect, like a typical Englishman, in preferring the game that hit him hardest. In his own happy way he was a glutton for punishment. He played football till he was well on the wrong side of forty and cricket till he had reached the wrong side of fifty. Then a very fast bowler struck him twice on the same knee and that hastened the declaration of his innings.

He learned his cricket in blood and tears, and those who believe that all human existence goes round in cycles may be interested to learn that the game's first impact on him (like its last) was a fearful blow on the knee-cap. The accident occurred at his prep school and, as he passed out, overwhelmed with the pain of it, little Arthur smiled happily. The blow had been struck by a popular professional cricketer, who was batting against the school at the time. What brought the victim complete rapture was the composite fact that he had been knocked silly by the mighty Tom Emmett and that Tom and his captain were reverently carrying him off to the school sanatorium.

Arthur's keenness on cricket at school shone brightly; when he reached medical school he could not give much time to the summer game, though he was able to play for his university at rugger, gaining a reputation as a fast, heavy forward. He did not flash with meteor flight into the cricket sky, as W.G. and E.M. had done, but worked his passage towards first-class status along some of the game's humbler, if more entertaining, by-ways. Against the Gentlemen of Warwickshire, for instance, he once took three wickets in three balls and, as a reward, was presented with a dainty little silver hat. This hat-trick was allowed to stand firmly in the records, despite his third victim's protest against alleged sharp practice. He had expected (he complained) the ball to come from the bowler's left hand and, when it came from the chap's right, he was completely put off his stroke. On another occasion, Arthur clean bowled a batsman of delicate sensibilities, who thereupon appealed, not to the umpire, but to the highest æsthetic canons: 'How can one bat against a fellow with a crude pink shirt-sleeve against a positively agonizing olivegreen background?'

In a not excessively serious international match at The Hague in the eighteen-nineties Arthur played a hero's part as a member of a wandering English eleven against a strong Dutch side which contained a genuinely redoubtable bowler. This was C. J. Posthuma, who may or may not have truly been, as his countrymen claimed, the Dutch W.G., but certainly enjoyed a reputation as the local equivalent of the Old Man. He was himself an amiable and lively character and the fact that he called his three dogs 'W.G.', 'C.B.' (after Fry) and 'Archie' (after A. C. MacLaren) was not the only evidence of his reasonable reverence for cricket. He showed his affection by coming over regularly to play for the side which W.G., in his later playing years, captained at the Crystal Palace and his name has a place of honour among London County's bowlers. In action Posthuma was a slow left-hander. He could endow the ball with a colossal break that could pitch off the locally laid matting and then, with a sudden lateral leap, whip in and shatter your wicket. Against a side capable of launching this dangerous assault, Arthur evolved an ingenious strategy: this involved exploiting his knowledge that the Dutch batsmen had been trained by an honest English coach to play everything 'straight' and never descend to anything which smacked of the agricultural inelegance of pulling. He therefore blandly packed his off-side with eager fieldsmen and had half the Dutchmen caught at cover. His delighted comrades carried him shoulder-high into the pavilion and then, having done him this honour, inconsequently dropped all sixteen stone of him.

Arthur played with J. M. Barrie's fantastic eleven, named by their captain the Allah-Akbarries, eccentric souls who had a note printed on their visiting cards:

Practice ground: Editorial Office, The National Observer.
This ground was chosen on the advice of Barrie, who forbade them to practise on their opponents' grounds as this could only give the opponents practice. In one of their matches Arthur came near to making eccentric history. The Allah-Akbarries had made 72 and had taken nine enemy wickets for exactly the same total. At this point Arthur started to bowl. There were indignant cries from the pavilion and the entire

batting side emerged, arguing fiercely. Arthur, you must understand, was the only effective bowler on the side and at this critical juncture, in sheer excitement and with no evil intent, he was beginning a new over, having just taken his ninth wicket with his last ball at the other end. For years afterwards Arthur claimed to be the first bowler who had attempted this felony (though by accident) and was a little hurt when a quarter of a century later Warwick Armstrong stole his thunder by breaking the same law in a Test match. In point of historic fact, Arthur was not allowed to bowl his second over, anyway. With all eleven opponents swarming round him, waving their copies of the Laws of Cricket, Arthur bowed to the storm and dropped his ball. To prevent a riot, another bowler was put on and the enemy won forthwith by a wide and four overthrows.

When Arthur finally deserted the Allah-Akbarries, his captain alleged, with a Captain Hook-like sneer, that he had gone into second-class cricket. This was, for the time being, literally true, and he played in minor county games with pleasure and some distinction. It was not until the first decade of the present century that Arthur achieved his boyhood's ambition of playing first-class cricket. When he played, it was not in odd games, but for the best part of the season, acquitting himself with credit against the leading counties, including Kent and Derbyshire, and finishing up at the end of August with the honourable batting average of 38. He took a modest pride in his ability to hold his place in a good M.C.C. side as an amateur bowler, because bowling in that period was almost invariably a professional's job. Just as J. T. Tyldesley was the only professional batsman to hold his own amid the fine flower of England's amateur talent, so Arthur, at an admittedly modester level, was one of the few amateur bowlers to win a place among M.C.C.'s hard-bitten pros. (Hesketh Pritchard was another, but that, as we shall see, is another story.) In time Arthur became one of the fairly select company who had bowled W.G. once, but confessed that, when he went in to bat in that particular game, the Old Man had his revenge.

Arthur liked to recount, for he had a certain talent as a story-teller, the tale of the three most disconcerting deliveries received by him during his first-class career. The first came from

W.G. himself. Arthur had with some pride put together a stylish thirty-odd runs, culminating in a handsome on-drive for four, and was stepping briskly out to take another boundary off the next ball. This delivery looked exactly the same as the one before, but the Old Man had cunningly flighted it so that it rose a little higher and dropped a little shorter. The instant Arthur moved, he was politely but remorselessly stumped by another Arthur—Arthur Augustus Lilley. That was a favourite ball of W.G.'s, child-like, bland, and deceitful as sin itself.

The ball that bothered Arthur even more than W.G.'s Chinese donkey-drop came to him in the form of a dive-bombing attack from A. P. Lucas, the eminent Cambridge, Essex and England cricketer, who should have known better. Somewhat incredibly, though Arthur was a truthful man, Lucas tossed up a thirty-foot lob, which would have been more at home at Wimbledon than at Lord's. As the ball came slowly but menacingly down, Arthur pondered deeply on the problem of defending his citadel against this dastardly attack from the skies. Oddly enough, it seemed easier to give it a name than to devise a plan for thwarting it, and, just as Tom Emmett had called his unplayable ball a Sostenutor, so Arthur thought of this thing, now descending, as the Spedigue Dropper. What should he do? Should he boldly attempt to drive it? Should he receive it more soberly by presenting the upturned face of the bat? The ball seemed an eternity in descending. At what seemed the last fraction of a moment Arthur changed his mind and unleashed a powerful and vindictive slash with the object of cutting the Thing past point. There was a crash of falling timber. Two stumps and the blade of his bat flew in different directions, and, as Arthur contemplated the wreckage, the ball descended mockingly on the remaining stump and knocked it sideways. Never, he reflected, had a batsman been dismissed so comprehensively.

The third most interesting delivery in his collection came from that tearaway fast bowler, that south-country Brearley, W. M. Bradley, of Kent. This particular ball rose violently and struck the batsman on the thigh. The pain was sharp, but natural. Quickly it sharpened and then became wholly unbearable.

'My word, sir,' murmured the wicket-keeper respectfully, 'you're on fire.'

Arthur clapped his hand to the spot. The ball, it appeared, had hit a small tin box of matches in his trousers pocket and ignited its contents. Whirling like a Dervish, Arthur snatched them out, hurled them as far from the crease as he could and, following with an agile spring, began to dance on them. W.G. lumbered in from point. 'Ho,' he chuckled in his beard. 'Couldn't get you out. Had to set you on fire.'

This seems the most exciting instance of incendiarism ever seen on a cricket field. Even Fiery Freddie never got a wicket by spontaneous combustion.

Arthur played cricket till long after this perilous escape; indeed, as long as his knee would let him. Years afterwards he wrote: 'I have had as long an innings as one could reasonably expect and carry many pleasant friendships and recollections away with me . . .'

He was a fine type of cricketing doctor. He had other accomplishments, too, possessing, as I have said, some talent for story-telling.

His full name—elementary, my dear Watson—was Arthur Conan Doyle.

CHAPTER 4

These were Good Men

I

A MAN'S faith is his own affair; he should be allowed to follow it in freedom and, if he wishes, in private. He may lead the good life and say nothing about it. Englishmen are notoriously diffident in these matters, and though a clergyman is licensed, both literally and metaphorically, to make a confession of his faith, it is exceptional for the layman to be granted any such licence by his fellows. He will have to give proof of the sincerity of his beliefs before he can claim their especial respect.

Of cricketing parsons there have been many in each of many generations and, with only one exception that I can think of, they have been good men. The Reverend Lord Frederick Beauclerk, who had a slightly fiendish temper and a habit of boasting that he made two hundred a year from gambling on the game, hardly qualifies as a man of virtue, though he scores full points as an eccentric.[1] His strength may have been as the strength of ten, but it is doubtful if his heart was pure. The cricketing parsons of my acquaintance, and one is a very famous cricketer indeed, have been, and are, men of the highest character, good Christians and good Englishmen. But sometimes you will find someone outside the clerical category who is equally a man of faith and integrity.

Cricketers, like other people, are of all sorts and conditions. and they would be the last men in the world to claim to be virtuous above their fellows. The attribution of mystical virtues to the game and those who play it is a besetting temptation to elderly schoolmasters and after-dinner speakers, but cricketers find it embarrassing. They know. I once heard a county captain say that he never cheated except against Glamorgan. I know, in fact, that he never cheated against anybody, but his attitude of mild (but crisp) cynicism was typical of the present age. Yet the modern cricketer, however cynical

[1] He was the only batsman who ever hung his gold watch on his leg bail.

his inclination, will always decently respect the sincerity of fellow-players like Johnny Lawrence and Dicky Dodds.

In Queen Victoria's reign (which the same I am free to defend) virtue was under no obligation to go underground. There were a few men out of whom goodness shone like a light. Such, in the second half of the nineteenth century, was Louis Hall, the Immortal Stonewaller. If you had called him a 'worthy' to his face, he would modestly have declined the compliment, but, however facetiously you may have used the phrase, he would somehow in time have made you feel a little ashamed of your facetiousness.

The great Lord Hawke was wont to recall that in the eighteen-eighties, when, as the Hon. Martin Bladen Hawke, he took over the captaincy of the Yorkshire eleven, they were a curious company: 'A fine lot,' said he, 'ten drunks and a chapel parson.' His lordship, it need hardly be said, spoke with humorous exaggeration. The ten of those days were by no means just 'drunks', though they counted in their ranks a few roistering companions and at least a couple of hard cases. He came nearer the mark with the eleventh, Louis Hall of Batley, for Louis, though not an ordained minister, held high lay office in the Methodist Church. He was a man of utter integrity, and I am using the word in its true sense; that is, his character was all of a piece. As a man and a cricketer, he stood four-square to all the winds that blew across the West Riding and its mill towns: solid, sober, infinitely patient and 'a desperate fellow to bowl at'. Frustrated attackers grumbled that bowling at Louis Hall was like plugging away at a laithe-door. His Christian name might reasonably have been pronounced in the usual way, but Batley folk knew better. For them, in their respectful affection and occasional exasperation, he was always 'Low-is'.

He began his cricket with a local lads' team which nobly, if portentously, called itself 'Rose of England'. Some of its members went to watch a match against the visiting All England Eleven and in practice at the nets before the game Louis clean bowled Hayward, which was about the contemporary equivalent of a Yorkshire schoolboy dismissing, say, Tom Graveney. 'This feat,' said Louis in the scriptural language which came so naturally to him, 'added a cubit to my stature.'

In his early days he had a small reputation as a tempting

and insidious bowler, a server-up of slow, round-arm donkey-drops. Old Joe Berry, a notable local character, laughed to scorn the very thought of such an artless attack. 'Fancy grown men getting out to that sort of stuff,' he muttered, as though the whole idea were childish. Nevertheless, Louis performed the hat-trick, and Joe was his third victim. Louis first had a trial for Yorkshire in 1873 when he was twenty, but he did not on this occasion set the Aire on fire and was not granted another chance till five years later. This call followed news of an innings played by him which was not so much an exhibition of batsmanship as a block of monumental masonry. Batting for the Eighteen of Hunslet and District against the touring Australians of that season, he defied every bowler they could muster, the mighty Spofforth and all. This innings set him on the right road. English cricket at that time *needed* men who could hold Spofforth at bay.

From the moment of his recall Louis became, and remained for seventeen years, the pillar and prop of the Yorkshire side. It is an historic fact that Yorkshire has often provided the backbone for England. Louis Hall gave backbone to Yorkshire. Like that later sturdy Yorkshireman, Maurice Leyland, he seemed to reserve his most enduring efforts for the hardest matches. Not for him the easy century against easy bowling on an easy wicket. His boldest front was reserved for the hereditary enemy. His highest score was made against Lancashire in a fierce Roses match in Jubilee year, and his tribute to Queen Victoria's fifty glorious years was a score of 160, as solidly built as a house of Yorkshire stone.

Throughout 1883 he was the leading professional batsman in the country; W.G. stood above all, but nobody else came near him. In recognition of this achievement, Batley determined to go to town. On Louis's return after the season's last match, the local brass band entered into a secret conspiracy to greet him at Batley station and play him home with Handel's *See the Conquering Hero Comes*. Brass bands, however, are among the objects which are hard to keep secret. Louis, if I may use the expression, got wind of the affair. He had never thought of himself as a conquering hero and so, with innocent cunning, he nipped out of the train at the previous station and quietly made his way home across the fields. But a Yorkshire brass band is not like the Lost Chord. It does not easily fade away into silence and it is undoubtedly loth to cease. Louis had hardly sat down to his tea when he heard them suddenly strike up in rousing style just outside his front door. Stricken with acute embarrassment, he was obliged to come out and make a speech. It was kind of them, he said, to blow their trumpets for him, because he was no hand at blowing his own.

In 1894, after a not particularly serious loss of form, he was obliged to retire from county cricket, 'to make way for the rising generation'. He accepted the end of this stage in his career with a philosophy that would be rarer to-day. 'Besides, I was forty,' he admitted, as though this were a slightly dis-creditable misfortune. 'It was fair enough . . .'

Apart from Scotton, his contemporary from Nottingham-shire, and perhaps Barlow of Lancashire, Louis Hall was the most famous stonewaller in the history of the game. He never quite attained, as did Scotton, the honour of a satirical parody in *Punch* ('Block, block, block . . .'). But he was solid enough. Compared with him, our friend Trevor Bailey would seem to be a reckless slasher. Hall's stonewalling was part, though only a part, of his cautious north country nature. When he had first played for Batley he had been a hard and frequent hitter, but, as Yorkshire's leading defender, he realized that the prime need was for solidity, and steadfastness became his watchword. His play was slow, but seldom dull, and his square cuts and fine glances were strokes for the eye of the connoisseur. Despite the slow pace of his scoring, he was seldom barracked, because it is not customary to barrack an institution. Besides, everyone, in Yorkshire at least, knew that he would always play for his side and not for himself, and he gave proof of this loyalty time and again. The facetious, who are always with us, admitted that he was a grand bat, because you could always pop out for a drink between hits. But his value to the side was immense. Others came and went. Louis stayed. He carried his bat through a Yorkshire innings seventeen times, and if it is not a record by any standard, then records have no meaning. It is a record, at any rate, for concentration and endurance. Again and again his resolution pulled Yorkshire out of the fire. His most patient performance was an innings which saved a county game at Canterbury by lasting two and three-quarter hours for twelve runs. He performed this feat of endurance, moreover, after spending a wretched night, prostrate with sea-sickness, on the return crossing after a match in Ireland. A fellow-townsman once dropped into poetry and sang his praises in stanzas which boldly rhymed sixer with elixir.

> *But give me the man who keeps 'em low,*
> *Who makes his honest fourers,*
> *Who in the crease keeps down his toe*
> *And troubles still the scorers . . .*

Louis kept 'em low and seldom hit sixers, but this did not mean that he was incapable of energetic action. Once, playing in a game for the United South against an Eighteen of Batley, W.G. tried every innocent-seeming subtlety in his repertory to lead the good man into temptation. Louis solemnly played every ball back to the bowler, but suddenly, without an instant's warning, he leaped into vehemence and hit a towering six over the square-leg boundary. The Old Man tugged at his beard, a recognizable sign of disapproval, but from that moment Louis played on sedately, as though this unseemly outbreak had been merely a thing of imagination, and spectators began to suspect that what they had seen was an optical illusion.

In company with George (Happy Jack) Ulyett, Louis Hall formed the first of those illustrious opening pairs with which Yorkshire has adorned and strengthened English cricket: Ulyett and Hall, Brown and Tunnicliffe, Holmes and Sutcliffe, Sutcliffe and Hutton, Hutton and Lowson, and (I am prepared to offer a modest wager) Stott and Taylor. Ulyett and Hall, the spiritual ancestors of all these happy couples, were as strikingly contrasted as any music-hall duo: Ulyett, the comedian, burly, boisterous, rubicund, and always laughing; Hall, in every sense the 'straight' man, sallow-complexioned, tall and slim with a slight scholarly stoop, serious of mien, his long features rendered even more melancholy by the heavy cavalry moustache of the period. Some photographs show him with his chin adorned by a smart 'imperial', an ironical touch, for never in history can two characters have been more strongly contrasted than the stable Louis and the unstable Louis Napoleon.

The Yorkshire pair were natural rivals to Lancashire's even more famous couple, Hornby and Barlow, heroes of cricket's greatest poem. Hall played the part of Yorkshire's Barlow, while Ulyett was Yorkshire's more ebullient Hornby. Their opening partnerships for their county were many and fruitful, and if Ulyett usually contributed the heavier share of the runs, he was almost always the first to go. Louis remained at his post, though the heavens might fall. (Perhaps from the boundary he looked so slow because Ulyett scored so quickly.) Louis was ever a tower of strength, not only in his batting, but in his personal influence. Sharp practice on the field, not wholly unknown in those days, became unthinkable in his presence. Even at the climax of a Roses match of unexampled ferocity, with the atmosphere still quivering at fever heat, he could with grave courtesy congratulate the Lancashire captain on his victory. The term 'Nature's gentleman', so often tossed about half-perfunctorily, half-cynically, shone out in its true meaning when bestowed on Louis Hall. On his retirement from county cricket he went to Uppingham to be coach to the school that has produced so many eminent cricketers, and among the boys he coached (and coached to some purpose) was Mr. T. L. Taylor, a great Yorkshire player in his active days and still president of the county club. At Uppingham Louis was able, without any difficulties in travelling, to attend chapel every Sunday. In his playing days he had made his way to his own chapel under considerable hardship. Matches then began on Mondays and Thursdays and getting home to Batley for Sunday often involved awkward travelling both before and after a match, but he never failed to make the journey. At Uppingham his weekly long-distance pilgrimages were over and he was now living only a few minutes' distance from the local Methodist chapel, so you can picture him leading his family to worship, immaculate in frock-coat and silk hat, his serious, kindly features serene in the sense of duty done.

When his coaching engagement ended, he went back to his native Batley, where he continued to devote his days to business and good works, taking, as by natural right, a leading part in the religious and political life of the town. He actually spent nine years in local government, being three times returned unopposed, for the simple reason that no one could be found to stand against him. No rival would have had a chance. In the council chamber, as at the wicket, he was calm, patient and, above all, prudent. He had always been careful not to throw his wicket away and this principle he applied with a benevolent rigidity to the council's finances. In his playing days he tended to avoid the expensive luncheon marquee and slip across the way for a penny cup of tea and a twopenny pork pie. But if publicly he favoured the frugal, in private he was the reverse. More than one old cricketer, down on his luck, had reason for gratitude to Louis Hall's generosity and pure goodness of heart. Often the suppliants owed their misfortunes to causes of which Louis could not possibly have approved, but that made no difference. He did not 'drink', he did not smoke, and he had a natural dislike of gambling, but, in an intolerant age, he was completely tolerant of those who disagreed with him. A kindly man may well help the unfortunate, but to help some detrimental old scallywag, for cricket's sake, and to refrain from lecturing him on his errors, that, it seems to me, is true and high virtue. It was only natural that he should have been one of the most active supporters of the Cricketers' Benevolent Fund, but this did not interfere with or detract from the good he did by stealth.

It had always been one of his principles—absurd to the present age, but worthy of respect—that he would neither buy nor read a Sunday paper, but when war broke out in 1914 and he heard the newsboys shouting, he capitulated. 'I think,' he said slowly, 'this is an occasion when I must have a Sunday paper.' It was a moment of the utmost solemnity. Louis had declared war on the enemy of mankind. He had broken the stern custom of a lifetime and for him, as for millions of his fellow-countrymen, nothing would ever be the same again.

He died in 1915, the same year as W.G. The country was engaged in a life-and-death struggle, but his town mourned him as its own possession. His old companions of the cricket field were among those who bore him to his last resting-place. With them was George Hirst, who had been a promising youngster at the time of Hall's retirement, and by the time of that sombre funeral had become Yorkshire's most mature and most typical professional. George Hirst never made a weak stroke, or bowled a careless ball, or spoke an insincere word. When he heard of Louis Hall's death, he wrote: 'He was a good man and his memory will long remain.'

And the rest of Louis Hall's deeds, and his 11,000 runs, and
all his not-out innings, are they not recorded in the book of
Wisden? As a man of his time, he belonged to three groups
which (as I think) are of inestimable value, but on which the
modern age might cynically pronounce the auctioneer's epitaph: he was a Methodist—*going*; he was a Liberal—*going*;
and he was a town councillor more careful of his fellow-
citizens' money than of his own—*gone*. But nothing can deprive him of Hirst's noble tribute:

He was a good man and his memory will long remain.

II

AT a first glimpse, it would be difficult to imagine characters
more sharply contrasted than Louis Hall, of Batley, and C. T.
Studd, of Eton and Cambridge. The two of them came from
what would now (rather horribly) be called different strata of
the nation's social and economic structure. They were as different from each other as the north and south of their country,
of which, both as men and as cricketers, they might have been
outstanding symbols. One of them, as we have seen, was slow,
defensive, tenacious in the Roundhead fashion, but more
tolerant; the other was a Cavalier, a 'cavalry' type of leader, a
dashing batsman, an inspired speaker and, in all his days and
ways, from his first Eton and Harrow match till his death in a
grass-roofed, mud-floored mission hut in the heart of Africa
fifty years later, he was a fiery spirit. Yet each of these two
men, so different in almost every way, had in common a deep
and abiding Christian faith. This faith Hall vindicated quietly
in his life of unselfish service and complete integrity; Studd
blazed a missionary trail round the world.

The most renowned of all cricketing brethren were without
question the Graces, E.M., W.G. and G.F. It might be argued
that an almost equally illustrious brotherhood came from
Worcestershire, sometimes known as Fostershire: H.K., R.E.,
W.L., G.N., B.S., M.K. and N.J.A. There is no arguing about
their quantity, and only a fool would argue about their
quality. Nevertheless, the brothers who came nearest in pattern to the three Graces were the three Studds, J.E.K. (Sir
Kynaston), G.B. (George) and C.T. (Charlie), the most famous
of them all. Closer to each other in age than the Graces, they

were all together in the Eton eleven in 1878 and in the extremely fine Cambridge eleven of 1880. (In the Winchester match of their common Eton year, they made 52, 53 and 54 respectively.) All the brothers were splendid all-round athletes and, even above the other two, C.T. was outstanding. He was school champion at fives and was extolled as 'incomparably the best cricketer on either side' in the Eton and Harrow match of 1879. Quite early in their lives, the brothers followed a natural religious bent and, whilst at Eton, started a class for Bible study.

Concentration is normally connected with defence, on the cricket field as elsewhere, but C.T. was patient in learning techniques to be used in attack. We know how W.G. learned the art of defence in the enchanted orchard at Downend. C. T. Studd learned to wield a straight bat by standing at a convenient distance from a long wardrobe mirror and moving his bat rhythmically along a seam of the carpet, so that in time the straightness of line would become automatic. Before going out to bat, he would stand with his eyes steadily fixed on a spot twenty-two yards away from him. By this means the length of the pitch was indelibly fixed in his judgment. Had he ever been a smoker, he would have given up the habit after his 'conversion' as a form of self-indulgence, but this did not arise. Like W.G., he had a dislike—almost a minor horror—of smoking. ('You can get rid of drink,' observed the Old Man, 'but you can't get rid of smoke.') C.T. believed that smoking affected an athlete's eyesight and, so strongly did he feel this, he would hurry away from the dining-room after dinner, when the cigars were brought out. In this way he sought to preserve the attacking player's highest asset, perfect sight. He was also dowered with another precious gift, wrists of steely strength. As an experiment, he had a bat made with a handle an inch longer than the normal, and when his powerful hands gripped this, his attacking power was enormous.

In 1881 he had a highly successful season at Cambridge, coming second in the University eleven's batting averages and third in the bowling. In 1882—mark the year—he reached the peak of his success. That season, in a near-classic age which saw W.G. and Alfred Lyttelton, Hornby and Barlow, Ulyett and Peate, and many others whose names were to remain legends for half a century, C.T. was the golden lad of English cricket. He scored exactly a hundred in the Gentlemen *v.* Players match, an honour which a happy few, but only a few, undergraduates have achieved; he made 126 not out for Cambridge against a strong Gentlemen of England eleven and 114 for the M.C.C. again Murdoch's Australians, the lean, grim fighters who later tumbled English cricket in the dust and reduced it to ashes; and, in what was his finest cricketing hour, he carried his University side to triumph against the same Australians.

It must have been one of the most dramatic contests ever staged against the placid backdrop of Fenner's. In the first innings, while ball fought bat every foot of the way, C.T. bowled destructively, taking five for 64 and, as if this was not enough, went in to bat with superb power and confidence. His score, which at the end of the first day reached 85 not out, roused the crowd to a pitch almost of exaltation, for, as *Wisden* primly observed, 'he was particularly severe on Spofforth', a majestic understatement which was rather like saying that Prince Rupert was a bit unkind to Cromwell's infantry. Here was magic before Ranji and thunder and lightning before Jessop. The crowd was bemused and enchanted, and so swiftly did rumours of his dazzling quality fly to and round London that in the morning excursion trains were run from Liverpool Street to give excited cricket lovers the chance of witnessing a whirlwind finish. (The old Great Eastern Railway is not often credited with swift and imaginative action. Gentlemen, let us honour the dead.)

The finish was as gripping as the most demanding excursionist could have wished. C.T. went on to bring his score to 118, and when Cambridge were all out the resilient Australians toughly recovered with a total that almost reached three hundred. Cambridge were left to get 168 to win, and it was plain from the first ball that every single run would have to be fought for. Horan, the old Australian cricketer-chronicler, muttered: 'We shall win if we can get that dam' set of Studds out!' But the Studds resisted extraction as if they had been fixed in an evening shirt, impregnably starched. J.E.K. and G.B. started off, as though the task were the easiest in the world, with 100 for the opening stand. Once G.B. was out, wickets began to fall quickly and the Australians once more asserted their grip upon the game. But the third Studd stuck fast. His score amounted to only 17 not out, but he extracted every run from the enemy with valour, sagacity and complete self-possession. After a final heroic battle for the very last run, C.T. carried out his bat. By six wickets Cambridge had conquered the invaders whom England could not conquer.

The year, as you will have noted, was the year of the most fateful and highly dramatized of all Test matches. In this game C. T. Studd played a part, but, owing to an historic, but none the less maddening, quirk of fate, it was hardly a hero's part. The story of the game has been told, both well and ill, oftener than that of any other and it shall not be told again here, except as it affects C.T. In the first innings he was clean bowled first ball by Spofforth, no doubt seeking demoniac vengeance for that 'particularly severe treatment'. Nevertheless, C.T.'s fielding did much to make amends for his batting failure. His swift pick-up and graceful return drew round after round of applause. Once an Australian batsman hit a ball towards Hornby in the deep and, following his team's agreed assumption that 'Monkey' could not throw for nuts, set off, good easy man, for an impudent run. Artfully, Hornby jerked the ball towards C.T. who, with lightning speed and precision, threw out his man by yards.

Everybody knows how, set 83 to win, England lost two wickets for a song (Oh, my Hornby and my Barlow!) and how W.G. and Happy Jack Ulyett courageously dragged England back from the edge of the abyss. The struggle was titanic, but they seemed to be winning it. With the score at 50 for two wickets the game appeared safe, but at this point Spofforth (probably at Spofforth's suggestion) was changed over to the pavilion end. From this moment wickets began to tumble in a crescendo of calamity. Ulyett went, caught at the wicket; W.G. went, after making one of his rare mishits. (Long afterwards he reminisced ruefully into his beard: 'I left six men to get 32 runs and they couldn't get 'em.') At 51 for four, there occurred a seemingly endless period, poised in space between the saturnine malevolence of the bowling and the suspended animation of the batting. While one batsman struggled with the Scylla of Spofforth, the other kept escaping, by the skin of his teeth, from the Charybdis represented by Boyle. Eighteen maiden overs rolled into eternity and then Spofforth struck again.

Tension in the pavilion was mounting. Studd was afterwards said to be a-quiver with nervousness, pacing the pavilion with a blanket wrapped round his shoulders, but all we know of the man, on the cricket field or anywhere else, suggests that this is an unlikely picture. He himself said, and no cricketer was ever a more truthful witness: 'The weather was cold and we sat in the committee room to keep warm.' (This, I think, accounts for the blanket.) It was during the interminable spell of maidens that there occurred to Hornby the cunning notion of changing his batting order. 'Do you mind, Charlie, going in lower down?' he asked. 'I want to keep you up my sleeve.' It is wildly improbable that any captain, least of all the thrusting and sagacious Hornby, would have thrust on to the bridge a Horatius riddled with neuroses.

So Charlie went up the sleeve and, alas for England, stayed there. Going in at No. 8, he waited at the bowler's end and watched two wickets fall quickly. Then came Peate, apparently determined to settle the fate of worlds with a couple of lusty blows. Though not an aggressively literate character, he may have determined, like the noble Montrose, 'to put it to the touch to win or lose it all'. He may, on the other hand, have felt with Charles Kingsley's three fishers: 'The sooner it's over, the sooner to sleep.' Off his first ball he hit a two; at the second he lunged insensately and vainly; the third bowled him hook, line and sinker. Studd had been sent on a sleeveless errand. He never received a ball. There remains only Peate's final observation, a classic contribution to history's doomsday book of famous last words.

'But why on earth didn't you play steadily, Ted?'

'Ah,' said Peate, 'I couldn't trust Mr. Studd.'

III

THE present time, the present place and the present writer are alike unsuited to describe the sudden change of heart which came upon the three brothers under the influence of the touring American evangelist Dwight L. Moody, a rich and colourful specimen for anyone's gallery of eccentrics. With fire

and zeal and a notable shrewdness, he preached his way round
our island, accompanied (in both senses) by his colleague, Ira
D. Sankey, the appealing singer of 'sacred songs and solos'. We
are entitled to our own opinions, respectful, realistic or painfully embarrassed, of American evangelism and particularly
of its more recent practitioners, but we cannot doubt the
Studds' sincerity. The force which struck them was as potent
as that which hurled Saul of Tarsus down in the dust of the
Damascus road. What happened to them could easily be explained by a modern psychologist—and he could easily be
wrong. What happened to J. E. K., G. B. and C. T. Studd will
be respected by those who understand it and *should* be respected by those who do not. C.T. did not give up cricket
right away; it may even be said that he never wholly gave it
up. After all, he was still an undergraduate. First he toured
Australia with Ivo Bligh's team which recovered the Ashes
lost at the Oval; then he enjoyed another happy season at
Cambridge, at the end of which he headed both the side's
batting and bowling. When he came down from Cambridge,
it was to give himself up to the new overmastering passion of
his life, the spread of Christian faith to darker lands.

His particular friend, Stanley P. Smith, who had been stroke
in the Cambridge boat, was another single-minded enthusiast
and the two of them became associate members of the China
Inland Mission. Two years later, reinforced by five companions, Studd and Smith sailed for China. 'The Cambridge
Seven' were on their way, as they said, to 'turn themselves into
Chinamen'. They went forth as the first disciples of the Gospel
went forth, supported by high faith but by very little else.
Literally they followed the injunction given by the Master to
the rich young ruler: 'Sell all thou hast and *give* . . .' C.T., in
one gesture of dedication, gave his private fortune; besides
smaller gifts, there were four cheques for £5,000 and five for
£1,000; of the larger cheques, one went to D. L. Moody and
another to George Muller, the founder of the orphanage which
looked out over the Gloucestershire county ground on Ashley
Down.

He attacked the difficulties of his work with all the force
and fire he had once expended on 'enemy' bowling. He was,
as we have observed, a natural leader of cavalry charges, a

Rupert of the mission-field. His first 'invasion' of China was a storm-trooper's attack; so was his whirlwind campaign ten years later through the American universities in search of student volunteers; so, too, was his historic journey between the Nile and Lake Chad fifteen years later still. He was an explorer for the same reason as Livingstone was an explorer: he was seeking new dark lands in which to spread the light.

His adventures were vividly reminiscent of St. Paul's: 'in journeyings often, in perils of waters, in perils by the heathen . . .' He spent the next six years in India, working, preaching, organizing with a kind of apostolic fury, and playing in occasional cricket matches, to the visible delight of his converts, who undoubtedly listened with added reverence to a preacher whom they had watched making double centuries. It may have seemed that he had a habit of dashing hither and thither starting work that he did not finish; but the criticism is not valid. Wherever he went, missions sprang up.

The final big adventure of his life was in Africa. Recuperating after an illness at home, he had determined to return to India when he saw a notice outside a Liverpool church: CANNIBALS WANT MISSIONARIES. This made him laugh; it also brought him into touch with the German missionary Karl Kumm, with whom he agreed to undertake a journey across Africa, eastward from the Niger, but, before they could start, malaria struck him down. He made a second plan to 'invade' Africa through Southern Sudan, but again his doctors (and his physical condition) forbade the move and, on the doctors' advice, his backers withdrew their support. This was a cruel blow. Penniless, broken in health and alone, he 'gambled' for God. He prayed, and in answer complete strangers sent him the money he needed for his next expedition across Sudan.

Was he a fanatic? Of course he was fanatical, but he was no stranger to laughter. At Khartoum he was entertained by the Sirdar, Sir Reginald Wingate, and if you dined with the Sirdar you had to dress. C.T.'s short sleeves were extremely short, but he did not accept defeat. Instead, he cut off the cuffs and pinned them inside his evening coat. I can imagine all sorts of comedy scenes that might have brightened the evening, but all passed in decorum. The next morning he was off into the interior, as though he were going on a holiday jaunt. Africa called him insistently and he lamented (though he did not often lament) that while many men would rush to exploit Africa for the sake of gold, few were hurrying to the task of turning Africa towards the true faith. Gathering a band of youthful workers around him, he named them 'God's Etceteras', as though they were a cricket touring side, and that, in a kind of smiling single-heartedness, was the kind of body they most resembled. Attended by only one of these young companions, he penetrated the dark hinterlands and the haunts of cannibal tribes, tramping in the footsteps of H. M. Stanley through the vast Ituri forest to Niangara, 'the very heart' of Africa.

He went through, and almost improved upon, that catalogue of perils of which the Apostle had nobly boasted: he survived envenomed snake bites; he settled tribal disputes in the spirit of a first-class umpire on behalf of the Colonial Office; he raised mission churches in clearings hacked out of the jungle; he fired revolver-shots into great rivers to scare off the crocodiles; he baptized drunkards, thieves, murderers and ex-cannibals; he had a devoted leading 'boy' who kept his canoe-crews at their work with the inspiring command: 'Get on, get on, I've eaten better men than you!' He built a church that was called the cricket-pitch church, because each side was twenty-two yards long. Every day he performed actions which were nine-tenths heroic and one-tenth ridiculous. Some early saints had the same gift. He did not mind if some people laughed at him; he could laugh at himself. Service should be given, he declared, not by dignified solemnity, but 'by reckless sacrifice and heroism'. He lived his later working life in a native hut and asked no better shelter. 'In weariness and painfulness, in watchings often, in hunger and thirst, in fastings often, in cold and nakedness . . .' In 1931 at Ibambi in the Belgian Congo he died, and the physical cause of death was that, though a desperately sick man, he would not consent to be bedridden. He could not believe that, just because he felt ill, the most important work in the world should be delayed. It was the final act of reckless sacrifice and heroism.

CHAPTER 5

My Hornby and My Barlow

I

ALWAYS excepting Queen Victoria herself, the most universally-acclaimed British institutions of the age that bears her illustrious name were William Ewart Gladstone and William Gilbert Grace. After these two great Williams, and always excepting the Royal Navy, probably the most cherished of our island's institutions was that rough, raucous home of the people's entertainment, the old English music hall. Dull would he be of soul in whom the sound of the music hall's great names—Marie Lloyd and Vesta Tilley, Dan Leno and George Robey, Harry Lauder and Little Tich—could not raise a flicker of interest. The man that hath no music hall in his soul is fit for treason, Hollywood and worse. Let no such man be trusted. . . . Within this happy institution was another curious institution, known as the Comedy Duo. I do not know who made the rules for such a combination, but they were fixed and immutable. The 'duo' consisted of a funny man and a 'straight' man, a comedian and his 'feed' or, as we should now call it, his stooge. The comedian would reinforce his efforts towards comedy with a bald wig, a bulbous red nose, patched and baggy trousers and elastic-sided boots the size of small canoes. The straight man was even more impressive, for he was the essence of correctitude. The evening suit which encased his frame recalled the glass of fashion and the mould of form; his silk hat, when he raised it, gleamed in the limelight. It would be churlish to object that his garb differed from the evening's customary suit of solemn black by being bright blue in colour. The general effect, in contrast to his companion's, was of strict normality.

This basic contrast between the 'funny' and the 'straight' is to be found in many walks and aspects of life, especially English life, but it is not particularly common on the cricket field. Cricket has had many famous partnerships, in both batting and bowling, but the contrast between the two who form them is not severe. (What, never? Well, hardly ever.) One bowler may be very fast and the other troublesomely slow; one batsman may be a little more exuberant and the other a little more subdued, but that will normally be all. That charming and penetrating writer, R. C. Robertson-Glasgow, once said of a famous Yorkshire pair that, while Sutcliffe looked as if he were about to lay a foundation stone at any moment, Holmes always had the air of a man perkily pushing off to the races. This was a pretty 'take' of verbal photography, but you will not find many such pictures.

Now, though this direct antithesis is rare, I can think of two others. One such pair we have already glanced at: Louis Hall, who played the chapel organ, and Ulyett, who kept a pub, each representing a side of life which I should hate to see disappear. England 'hath need' of both. Even more delightfully contrasted were the heroes of cricket's greatest poem, Lancashire's great twin brethren, 'my Hornby and my Barlow long ago'.

II

BARLOW was the straight man, the sturdy professional, sober, slow, resourceful and steady; Hornby was the inspired amateur, excitable, dashing, immensely combative and slightly outrageous. He was an England rugger three-quarter (nine caps) and he tackled cricket *like* a rugger player. He had a good deal in common with E. M. Grace, for he was on the small side and made up for his lack of inches by a determination to fight any enemy in sight. Like E.M., he was capable of chasing a barracker twice his size out of Old Trafford, and also like E.M., he rode to hounds in winter, hard and straight as an arrow. If he did not like what a sports writer had said of him, he did not pen him a pained note. He did not write to *The Times*, pleading for higher standards of objectivity in sporting journalism. He simply darted up the steps of the old Press Box at Old Trafford, seized the feller by the collar—anybody who offended Hornby was always 'the feller'—and ran him downstairs, out of the ground, and probably out of Manchester altogether. Why he was not regularly sued for assault and battery

I cannot imagine. Perhaps the consciences of his victims told them that their punishment had been well deserved. But I doubt it.

At Sydney in 1879 he quelled a riot single-handed. The crowd, incensed by an umpire's decision—he was a Melbourne umpire—about a run-out, surged on to the field bent on attacking the English team. It was an ugly moment and the players moved into position for self-protection and to defend their captain, Lord Harris. As the ringleader struck out at Lord Harris with a stick, Hornby grabbed him by the scruff of the neck and propelled him like a wheel-barrow towards the pavilion. The crowd practically ripped the shirt off his back, but he got his man, not only into the pavilion but into the hands of the police.

When he first battled his way into a Harrow eleven full of fine batsmen, he was said to weigh only six stones, 'bat and all'. I do not believe this statement for a moment, but, if it is true, they were six stones of steel, whipcord and bounding energy. His nickname, 'Monkey', attached itself to him not so much because of any monkeyish cast of feature as from a frankly impish quality in his nature. All his humour was either sardonic or puckish. When he was proffered sympathy for being dismissed by a monstrously high catch by the long-armed William Gunn leaning back over the boundary-rail, he murmured: 'Only a dam' giraffe could have got near the thing.'

Lancashire enjoyed one of its several ascendant periods under his captaincy. In his first two years as leader they played twenty-four matches and lost only one. True, providence had sent him some wonderful material to work on, material of the quality of A. G. Steel, Barlow and Johnny Briggs. Pilling was the most agile wicket-keeper of his period and the Rev. Vernon Royle the most dashing cover-point. ('Don't run,' said Tom Emmett, 'there's a p'liceman there.') Individually, all the eleven were highly gifted players, but without Hornby at their head they could not collectively have been so formidable. He had himself forged the weapon and was himself its warhead. Just as, physically, he took the barracker by the collar, so, metaphorically, he would seize his opponents by the scruff of the neck and sweep them into the dustbin. His grip on any match in which he took part was relentless. Thus

did he lay the foundations of that hard but effective school for
captains in which the eventual pupils were masterful skippers,
like Brian Sellers in the north and Stuart Surridge in the
south.

In the field his tactics were almost uniformly triumphant,
though, as we noted, his plan in the notorious Ashes Test to
'keep Charlie up his sleeve' came unhappily to grief. He captained England twice: the other, less fateful, game was the
drawn match at Old Trafford in 1884. His half-dozen Test
innings did not add up to more than twenty-one runs, and
this in another batsman would have spelt failure, but there
are some qualities which cannot be reckoned in figures. His
force and inspiration, indeed his mere presence in the side,
were worth more than a hatful of runs. Ever a fighter, for him
the true pleasure of the game was the joy of battle. He feared
no man's frown and was one of the few who could face the
formidable W.G. without awe. A tussle with W.G., employing
bat, ball and sheer force of character to the top of its bent,
was meat and drink to 'Monkey' Hornby. I will go further
and declare that Hornby was the one cricketer who never gave
ground, even to W.G. and E.M. in combination. If they glared
at him he could glare back and treat those two past-masters
just the same . . .

The best-remembered lines in Francis Thompson's poem,
As the run-stealers flicker to and fro, to and fro, draw their inspiration from Hornby's diabolical *penchant* for running
short runs, which kept spectators (and his unfortunate partners) in a fever of mingled delight and terror. His partners, indeed, dismayed as they were by his tactics, might well have
cried out with the Duke of Wellington: 'They may not
frighten the enemy, but, by gad, they frighten me!' Fieldsmen
were continually persuaded to believe that they could run him
out, which happened seldom; they had more sporting chances
of running his partners out, which happened frequently. If the
attacking side ever managed to get rid of him, they would
murmur with mock-wistfulness: 'What a pity Mr. 'Ornby's
out; we shall have to *bowl* the other ones!'

In his own book on cricket, W.G. recalled how in one of
the old Gentlemen *v.* Players games he and Hornby, instead
of trying to punish the bowling and make as many runs as

they could, played tip and run for half an hour and reduced the morale of bowlers and fieldsmen to a wobbly jelly. Each batsman vied with the other in crazy calls. Even Denis Compton would have shown greater discretion. W.G. stopped a ball dead in front of him and, without looking where it went, yelled: 'Come on, Monkey!' Quick as W.G. had been, Hornby was quicker. He was up like a lightning flash, before the words were out of the Old Man's beard. The ball rolled straight up the pitch to the bowler, Willsher of Kent, who ran forward to meet it. W.G., though he thought he was a goner, determined to keep on running, and Willsher, hearing the Old Man's bulk thundering behind him, lost his head and, although he might easily have removed the bails without fuss, he hurled the ball with all his might—yards wide. 'This,' said W.G. with a straight face, 'was the culminating point of our temporary insanity; for Mr. Hornby and I were so tickled at the absurdity of the run attempted that we settled down and played correctly . . .'

The run-stealing of Hornby and Barlow was not that smooth, well-oiled, relentless machine as perfected by Hobbs and Rhodes and afterwards by Hobbs and Sutcliffe. The secret of this technique Wilfred Rhodes explained, as always, with a straight face: 'When we're comin', we say Yes, and when we're staying, we say No . . o.' It would be over-simplifying to say that the Hornby and Barlow method was just the opposite. It was much more complicated than that. But sometimes, on a bellow of 'Come on, Dick!', both batsmen would dash madly up the pitch and just as madly back again, with the result that a demented fieldsman would hurl the ball over the wicket-keeper's head for four overthrows. At another time, Hornby would solemnly intone: 'Stay there, Dick,' and those two wicked batsmen would slip along the length of the pitch as swiftly and silently as goldfish darting along the side of a tank. But you never knew; you never really could tell. That is why so many of Hornby's partners were run out and why even the patient Barlow protested: 'First he runs you out of breath, then he runs you out and then he gives you a sovereign.'

Though famous as a run-stealer, Hornby was entitled to the greatest respect as a punishing run-getter. What was remarkable was not so much his tip-and-run tactics as his persistent, hard and relentless driving. He was a hitter, but never a mere hitter. His scoring was swift and his centuries were seventeen; in his best years he was good enough to be a serious rival to W.G.

When, after more than thirty years of supremely active service, nearly twenty of them as captain, Hornby retired in favour of S. M. Crosfield, and then A. C. MacLaren, he could truly say he had fought the good fight, for every game in which he took part was a battle. But not necessarily a grim one . . .

III

RICHARD GORTON BARLOW, it need hardly be insisted, was different and complementary, particularly in his humour. Whereas Hornby's humour was gay and boisterous, even obstreperous, Barlow's, unlike the climate of his native Bolton, was very dry. He would report with solemn face the observation alleged to have been made by an Old Trafford spectator: 'I'm glad to see t'back of 'Ornby; he's never happy till he's got Barlow run out.' After a match against Leicestershire in which he had carried his bat through the innings for 29, remaining rooted at the wicket for three and a quarter hours, he attended a dinner and smoking concert given to the players and sang, with feeling, *You'll Remember Me*. It was his particular humour to wonder why the audience laughed so uproariously.

Some cricketers when they tramp off the field at close of play like to leave cricket behind them. It is a point of view. Barlow belonged to the contrary school: he ate and drank cricket and no doubt talked cricket in his sleep. When he retired from the county eleven, he became a first-class umpire, and when he gave up umpiring he ran a sports shop. The house in Blackpool which he had built for his retirement was as much an oddity as the nearby Tower. From front porch to attic, it was a cricket museum. In a panel of the inner front door, he and Hornby appeared like saints in a stained-glass window with Dick Pilling crouching behind them in pads and gloves as a guardian angel. Along the wall of the bathroom hung an austere row of bats. With one of these he had made 4,000 runs. Another he had carried through the innings seven times. It would have been difficult to take the quickest bath in that house without succumbing to profoundly solemn thoughts.

Barlow, unlike most members of the county side, was a true Lancastrian—most of them, it was wickedly alleged, were recruited from Nottinghamshire—and he fittingly received his baptism of fire in a Lancashire *v*. Yorkshire match. In this game he took a wicket with his first ball in county cricket. He also carried out his bat for 28 with a bandaged hand. He did not confess till afterwards that he had been batting with a fractured finger.

In 1882, the year of the calamitous Ashes match, he topped his county's averages in both batting and bowling. No Lancastrian had ever done this before, and I cannot remember that any wearer of the red rose has done it since. It is one of the misfortunes of history that some ill deeds gain a maximum of publicity and that many good deeds miss their chance of shining in a naughty world. Of that Test match we have heard much—perhaps too much—of its failures and disasters, but few people remember that in Australia's first innings Barlow took five wickets for 19. This bowling was almost as devastating as Spofforth's in the same match. There is no higher praise.

Barlow claimed that the word 'stonewaller' was first applied to himself by William Barnes, of Notts, who had bowled at him for two and a half hours while scoring five runs. 'By gow, Dick,' said Barnes, 'bowling at thee were like bowling at a stone wall!' And that is how stonewallers were born. But Barlow, though the first stonewaller named as such, was not always behaving like the Abominable Slow-man. He once hit three fours in an over at Lord's and in a game at Stockport drove the ball into a neighbour's potato-field, where it was lost for ever. He even struck, of all persons, Louis Hall, on the head at silly mid-on. (The bowler had said: 'Get thee in a bit, Lowis. Barlow won't hurt thee.') For one horrid moment Barlow thought he had killed him and was absurdly relieved when Louis rose with dignity to state in his usual courteous, but determined, voice that silly mid-on had seen the last of him.

Ten years later Barlow found himself at the crease in another Yorkshire *v*. Lancashire match and saw the face of George (Happy Jack) Ulyett, bland and cheerful, smiling at him from silly-point. To add insult to injury, Ulyett picked the first ball sent down off the edge of the bat as though it were a ripe cherry. Barlow walked slowly back to the pavilion, thinking sombre thoughts. At that moment he could have cheerfully murdered his friend. When he came in again for his second innings, Ulyett was still standing at the fatal spot, smiling, as though he had never moved. If Barlow had known the language of the cinema-goer, he might have observed: 'This is where I came in . . .'

'Now, George,' said he, speaking as one reasonable man to another, 'would you mind stepping back? I shouldn't like to kill thee.'

'Well, Dick,' replied Ulyett equally reasonably, 'if tha does, it'll be t'first time tha's ever killed with hard hitting.'

In the next over there came down a loose ball on the off and Barlow cut it with all his strength. The next thing he saw was Ulyett tossing it up in the air. Ulyett was that sort of person. Barlow's control of temper was splendid. He walked slowly away with a rueful smile. 'Ah, well, George,' he said, 'th'art master to-day. But wait . . .'

He toured Australia three times: first under Alfred Shaw and Arthur Shrewsbury in 1881–82; secondly with Ivo Bligh's team which went out to recover the Ashes as soon as they had been lost; and thirdly, with Shaw and Shrewsbury in the successful tour of 1886–87. The team which undertook the second tour had a horrifyingly near escape from extinction when their ship was run down in the Indian Ocean by a sailing ship which had wandered off her course. The tourists' ship was holed, but mercifully the gash was five feet above the water-line, and the sea remained calm. So, after the initial shock, did the cricketers who, with their four hundred fellow-passengers, were brought back to Colombo in safety. For most of them the collision was a nine days' wonder; for one man it was a tragedy. This was Fred Morley, the Notts fast bowler, who received a nasty blow at the moment of impact. He suffered great pain and, on examination when the team reached Melbourne, he was found to have several ribs broken. This made it impossible for him to play on the tour, and the voyage home brought no relief; a more serious illness set in and he died soon after landing. It is a sad story and Barlow felt deeply about it.

The modern cricketer may well blench in pained incredulity to know that Barlow played in every match of all three of his Australian tours. In the last match of the last tour he had a damaged foot and batted with a runner, thus preserving his unique record. The marvel is that he did this and lived to tell the tale. He even played, on the first tour's outward journey, in the famous match at San Francisco, in which a locally famous baseball pitcher bamboozled the English batsmen in the first innings, but was remorselessly ill-treated by them in the second. Some rather naughty gambling went on, of which Louis Hall would not have approved. Ulyett and Barlow—the idea must have been Ulyett's, for he was the betting man of the party—accepted odds of twenty to one in half-crowns (this was presumably before the dollar became excessively hard currency) from all comers who maintained that the two of them would not make a hundred for the first wicket. They put on 166 and a tidy sum of money changed hands. The journey out had been as rough as any cricketers had ever endured. Once when Barlow and Tom Emmett were left alone in the saloon, the ship gave such an almighty heave that Barlow involuntarily grabbed the edge of a clamped-down table and pulled with might and main until the ship righted herself. He repeated his action with each successive roll until he came to believe that he had saved the ship from foundering. Or so Tom Emmett said . . .

Though Barlow's splendid bowling was not quite penetrative enough to save the Ashes match at the Oval, he had a strong conviction that his feat of taking seven wickets for 40 in the third of the 1882–83 Tests against Australia was by far his best performance and a paramount contribution to the regaining of the Ashes. Australia, after a stonewalling effort by Alec Bannerman worthy of Barlow himself, were set 153 to win in the fourth innings and on a damaged wicket our hero virtually destroyed them. He was pleased to have bowled so well and delighted to have helped England to a victory that was to wipe out the sting of defeat; he appreciated the silver cup his friends were getting ready to give him and the generous collection they were making for him. What genuinely scared him was the fact that his cheering admirers were rushing towards him with a view to seizing him and carrying him off the field shoulder-high. There was no escape and they got their man. To a man with the dignity and portly presence of Barlow, this was acutely embarrassing and he was not quick enough to cry (as did Tom Emmett in a similar predicament): 'Nay, lads, put me down. All t'brass is tumbling out o' my pockets.'

Barlow was also haunted by a previous adventure at home when he and Hornby had won a great victory for Lancashire by scoring 148 on a rough wicket in the fourth innings of the match without being parted. The instant the winning hit was made, the Manchester crowd surged on to the ground and the heroes ran for their lives. In 1875 the players' dressing-rooms at Old Trafford were much farther from the pitch than the gentlemen's and, while Hornby got away, Barlow was caught, lifted up, and carried in triumphantly. That sort of experience leaves its mark upon a man. It is a final argument, if one were needed, against separate dressing-rooms for amateurs and professionals.

CHAPTER 6

Bat, Ball and Boomerang

I

THE All Blacks of 1905, that formidable phalanx of Rugby footballers from New Zealand, were the first Commonwealth visitors to go by that name, but the title might have been more reasonably claimed by the cricketing 'all blacks', that first visiting side from Australia of thirty-seven years earlier, who, apart from their captain, Charles Lawrence, who was also their manager, were Aborigines to a man. In comparatively recent years, only three Aborigines have played State cricket: A. Henry, 'Eddie' Gilbert and J. J. Marsh, the first two of them for Queensland and the third for New South Wales. Of the three, only Gilbert lent much colour to the game. The two best-known facts about him are: (1) his speed was so furious that he once knocked the bat clean out of Bradman's hands and (2) Learie Constantine hit a very fast ball from him out of the Woollongabba ground at Brisbane. They never found the ball. Knowing Constantine, I fancy it may have reached the Great Barrier Reef.

In the eighteen-sixties, however, there were more Aborigines in the game, and in the side that Lawrence brought over there were thirteen. Lawrence himself was a remarkable cricketer. He played at different times for Middlesex and Surrey, and undertook professional engagements in both Scotland and Ireland. Playing for a Scottish Twenty-two against the All England Eleven he bowled Julius Cæsar so comprehensively that all three stumps were knocked out of the ground. I should have thought this hardly physically possible, but the records are firm and clear. He went out to Australia with H. H. Stephenson's team and, when they came home, he stayed on to coach the Albert Club, Sydney's leading cricket combination. It was he who conceived the idea of the tour undertaken by his pupils. The visit, like all early tours, was an effort of private enterprise, and, on Lawrence's persuasion, was backed by four gentlemen of speculative temperament, headed by a Mr. Graham, of Sydney.

You can see the portraits of the Aborigines, built up into a composite picture, in the Imperial Cricket Museum at Lord's. They were members of the Werrumbrook tribe, a race then living in Victoria but now extinct, and in its day very different in character from the present-day Aborigines of Northern Queensland, with which modern ethnological research, benevolent social work and the delightful detective stories of Arthur Upfield have made us familiar. Our cricketing Aborigines, it is claimed, were nearer in race to the Maoris of New Zealand, though their photographs hardly seem to support this theory. Frankly, they are not as handsome as Maoris, but nothing could now matter less.

Their photographs show them to be black, bearded and, with one or two exceptions, wiry rather than muscular. Their costume is fascinatingly varied. Some are clad in unexceptionable flannels; others appear to be wearing shorts over their trousers. (Who would presume to be fashion's arbiter in such matters?) Their feet are bare. Only a few bear (or brandish) the simple implements connected with their cricket. Mullagh carries a bat over his shoulder and is well within his rights in doing so, for he was by far the best batsman, not to mention the best bowler and wicket-keeper, in the side; Johnny Cuzens, the second-best bowler, is shown in the act of delivering a deadly ball, and Red Cap, in a solemn manner which he seldom assumed in real life at the crease, is squaring up defensively. All the others are provided with examples of their true native weapons: boomerangs, spears and a curious narrow shield, in shape rather like a pelota-basket. Some of them are adorned with gay sashes, just as footballers wear numbers, to distinguish their identities,[1] and the colours—maroon, pink, yellow, magenta—all added to the brightness of the scene.

Apart from polar explorers, our Aborigines must have become in time the most harassed (or hardened) of travellers. They endured a sea voyage of inordinate length on the *Paramatta*, not the kindliest of ships, but this was no unkinder than what came later. They took up their first headquarters at Town

---

[1] Except at Cardiff Arms Park, where the mud renders this impossible.

Malling in Kent. Afterwards, they moved into a pub called the Queen's Head in the Borough and seemed to have found London less idyllic but more congenial.

At first, because of a prejudice, not against the colour, but against the sheer strangeness, of the visitors, the business of planning their fixture list hung fire, but the M.C.C., in characteristically courteous and helpful fashion, came forward and offered them a game at Lord's. After this became known, fixtures in plenty were showered on them. They might possibly have complained that their fixtures were imperfectly arranged, but no one could say that a total of forty-seven matches was insufficient.

Their first game took place at the Oval. It was not played against the county side, which in those days of H. H. Stephenson, George Griffith and Billy Caffyn would no doubt have been too strong for them, but against an excellent Gentlemen's side, the Surrey Club. The Club, who batted first, eventually won by an innings, but the Aborigines put up a stiff enough resistance to show they had good quality in them. Lawrence, of course, helped to give the side a certain stiffening, but splendid batting in each innings came from Mullagh, whose keenness and success were to last right through the tour.

After this game the Aborigines gave a quite electrifying display of spear and boomerang throwing, the *grand finale* of which was a contribution by Dick-a-Dick, who allowed five gentlemen of Surrey, including Mr. William Burrup, the county's honorary secretary, to pelt him with cricket balls as hard as they could go. It sounds an ungentlemanly thing to have done, but everybody, including Dick-a-Dick, swaying, swinging and dodging fantastically, seems to have enjoyed it.

Several interesting things happened to the Aborigines at the Oval that day. Mullagh, because of his unexpectedly brilliant batting, was awarded a golden sovereign as talent money, formally presented by the Surrey secretary in front of the pavilion. Among those who took part in the sports with the Aborigines was a lanky young fellow, just short of his twentieth birthday, who had come up from Bristol to try his hand at throwing the cricket ball. In three goes he threw 116, 117 and 118 yards and, at his fourth attempt, he threw the ball 109 yards one way and 104 the other. His name was William Gilbert Grace, and whether he was acclaimed the winner of this particular competition I do not know.

After the game the visitors were joined by William Shepherd, a young member of the Surrey ground staff who had stood umpire for them. He became a valuable addition to the side, helping with the general management, umpiring and captaining the eleven when Lawrence took a rest.

Some 7,000 watched the game and about half of them stayed to see the sports. The Aborigines were subsequently taken to see the Derby at Epsom. They missed Hermit's Derby by a year, but I hope they found the winner at equally long odds.

II

So they were launched upon their arduous Odyssey which lasted from 26th May until the third week in October, and for sheer strenuousness I can think of nothing to compare with it except the Maori rugger team, brought over in similar circumstances in the eighteen-eighties, and condemned to a programme of seventy matches that a galley-slave would hardly have considered leisurely. Our Aborigines played forty-seven matches, won fourteen, lost the same number and drew nineteen. It is to their credit that most of their losses were incurred early on, before they had had a chance of getting used to English conditions. Indeed, when you consider the sheer wear and tear of their itinerary, it is highly to their credit that they won any matches at all.

It was the day-to-day travelling that they found most punishing. Nobody knows if any of them when at home had ever followed the Aboriginal custom of 'going walkabout', but their stay in England was one long 'walkabout'. Try to imagine forty-seven unco-ordinated journeys, including trips between such far-flung places as Kennington and Keighley, Plymouth and Tynemouth, Brighton and Bootle. Shepherd, a sharp-eyed, good-natured little man, mopped his brow in the fierce heat of England's hottest summer for many years, and wondered why these journeys, so ill-arranged and costly, could not have been put into the hands of some more intelligent wanderer. Why, for instance, had they not consulted George Parr, captain and manager of the All England Eleven, who had been touring the cricketing towns for years, and whose knowledge of the tricks of transport might have saved the managers much money and the players much discomfort? Even under these hardships the 'demeanour of the Blacks was most becoming' and they travelled from Rochdale to Swansea and from Swansea to Bradford without a murmur. Perhaps they were sustained and uplifted by the fact that at Bootle a boomerang was swung off course by the wind and decapitated a spectator's tall hat.

For publicity's sake, the circus always put up at the best hotels and, at this distance of time, it is impossible not to be awed by the thought of Bullocky, Dick-a-Dick and Jimmy Mosquito flaunting it in the best hotels in Hunslet, Rochdale and Bootle. This, it was complained, played havoc with the venture's finances.

The two leading accounts of the tour are not agreed upon its financial results. One, quoting the large crowds which the visitors attracted everywhere by their enterprising cricket and especially by their athletic displays, declares it to have been a success. The other authority, our Mr. Shepherd, argued otherwise. Indeed, Shepherd, whose business acumen should have stamped him as a Scot or a Yorkshireman instead of a mere Southerner, demonstrated in relentless Micawber-like economic logic how the tour lost £2,000, a deficit which should have been shared by four speculators, but fell in fact most heavily upon the unfortunate Mr. Graham of Sydney, who had planked down the money in the first place. This loss, and doubts for the future that it spread, put an end to the plan which Lawrence had conceived of wintering in the south of France and returning the following season. The money risk was too heavy.

III

BESIDES a well-patronized game against the M.C.C. at Lord's, in which Mullagh again distinguished himself with both bat and ball, the Aborigines made spasmodic forays into Kent and East Lancashire and had some gruesome experiences at Turnham Green on a truly rural wicket, which consisted wholly of ridge and furrow.

Not all the players enjoyed equal success throughout the tour. Easily the most dexterous was Johnny Mullagh, who made

1,670 runs and took nearly 250 wickets, an impressive season's performance by anybody anywhere. Not content with such an excellent record, he frequently kept wicket as a substitute for Bullocky, the regular practitioner, and took a toll of forty victims, half of them stumped. His bowling was of the old-fashioned honest sort, fast and straight. He reinforced his formidable quality by moving swiftly towards the batsman as he finished his delivery, just as W.G. habitually trotted towards silly mid-off. The result was that a surprising number of batsmen found themselves first mesmerized and then caught and bowled. An even bigger number were run out by his swift, deadly aim.

Johnny Cuzens, another remarkable athlete, came next highest among the records both for batting and bowling. His bowling action was not unlike that of some other bowlers we could name; it was, they say, 'of the windmill description'. His deliveries were menacingly fast and bumpy and the manner in which he exploited the relaxed rule about raising the arm above the shoulder is just nobody's business. Conservative old gentlemen who had muttered darkly about the thin end of the wedge were beginning to say: 'I told you so', but the authorities were past worrying about this now. Over-arm bowling had come to stay. Johnny Cuzens also made his thousand runs and took his hundred wickets and was probably the side's best sprinter. It was his habit to run barefoot until the solicitous Mr. Shepherd had a pair of special running pumps made for him in Sheffield. On the third day of the last match of their tour Cuzens was challenged by an anonymous sprinter from the north. Shepherd, who suspected some jiggery-pokery in the wager, was disposed to frown on the challenge, but the tourists' London host happened to be William Holland, proprietor of the old Canterbury music hall, who was full of admiration for his guest. Holland was a man of large ideas and was what we should now call publicity-minded. He once proposed to place an outsize carpet, value at £1,000, in the vestibule of his music hall and was undeterred by the suggestion that patrons would only spit on it.

'Fine,' said he. 'We'll advertise in the papers: "Come and spit on our £1,000 carpet".'

Nothing could stop him from offering to put a fiver on

Johnny Cuzens and, almost before Shepherd could open his mouth in protest, the race had started. Cuzens sent his supporters' hearts into their mouths by being slow off the mark and subjected them to something near thrombosis when, half-way down the track, he kicked off one of his running pumps. But from that instant he moved like the wind and slipped past his rival. As he breasted the tape he was engulfed in the warm embrace of his chief backer who, true to the open-handed tradition of the music hall, pressed both stake and winnings into the runner's hand.

Bullocky was a courageous wicket-keeper with a granite frame and would have kept just as boldly unarmed by pads or gloves. He was also a stubborn bat, sometimes exasperatingly so, and had one heroic innings of 64 not out at Hastings which would have done credit to the last of the Saxons.

The rest of the Aborigines, though keen fielders and good sportsmen, were fair-to-indifferent performers with bat and ball. One of their drawbacks (if drawback is the right word) was that they showed a certain rashness in hitting and something more reprehensible than rashness in running between the wickets. To such a degree was their judgment at fault that on the tour there were nearly sixty run-outs. Is this, you may well ask, a record? Twopenny, despite the fact that his sash was drab in colour, was a hearty smiter of what we should now call the 'Jim Smith' school, and performed a feat which I do not think either Grace or Bradman ever achieved: he once hit a 9 (repeat nine) all run and without benefit of overthrow. I hope that news of this feat can be kept from Messrs. Wardle and Trueman, who might spend the rest of their active (and otherwise blameless) lives in striving to emulate it.

The Aborigine named Sundown played in only two matches and, despite rival historic claims, must have been the original hero of the legend: 'In the first innings he made one and in the second he was not so successful.' There is an air of Odyssey about the thought of a man travelling right round the world (once round the Horn) for the pleasure of making one run. What is even odder is that he had never made a run in a match before the tour and that he never made a run when he got back home. It is no cliché to say that he never 'troubled the scorers'. Poor Sundown. Or should we say: 'Happy Sundown'?

Perhaps it is better to travel hopefully towards the supreme ambition of breaking your duck than to arrive, and he remains a magnificent example of hope and endurance to all the worst batsmen in the world. (Was he by any chance a bowler or a good fielder? And it is interesting to ponder on the stroke that brought him the one historic run: can it, for instance, be proved beyond question that the shot was intentional?) The triumphs of Peter were much more spectacular. His tale of forty-two matches was studded with seventeen ducks. Old Jemmy Shaw of Notts never did anything half so clever. Even among the bowlers who took more wickets in their careers than they scored runs, this remains an impressive achievement. I doubt if even Eric Hollies could show so proud a record.

IV

IN his capacity as guide, philosopher and friend to the visitors, Mr. Shepherd did a thorough season's work, chivvying his flock to their games with all the ardour and persistence of a good-natured sheep-dog. His favourite was Dick-a-Dick, a true eccentric with an aristocratic ignorance of the value of money. It was his pleasure to waste his substance on riotous living, as exemplified by the hoop-la stall and wheel of fortune at local fairs and bazaars. Whatever money he had earned, he risked every penny of it, with a gambler's passion, on the prizes that such side-shows dispense. These were mainly of the china-ornament or pot-dog variety, and can have been no less hideous than the rest of their kind. Their æsthetic appeal for Dick-a-Dick, however, was strong. The prize that appealed to him most was a Swiss alarm clock. It cost him anything up to ten times its value to win it and, once won, he carried it under his arm practically every moment of the tour. Shepherd had to wind it up for him each day.

Once Dick-a-Dick introduced drama into the humdrum routine of travel. The eleven were peacefully assembled in the railway station of a West Riding town, waiting for their train. Suddenly Dick-a-Dick broke away from them and bolted. Lawrence, who thought his protégé was on the point of running amok, made a wild, but vain, effort to grab him. Dick-a-Dick was the best hurdler in the team, and the sight of a tall, lean black man determinedly hurdling through the streets of Dewsbury must have given the inhabitants a rare treat. It may even have disturbed one or two of the inhabitants out of their native imperturbability, inducing at least one of them to murmur: 'Ee, you don't see so much of that sort of thing nowadays.' Dick-a-Dick was seen to dash into the hotel and dash out of it again, a happy smile on his face and the precious clock, which he had in a moment of aberration left behind, now safely under his arm. The train was late, so Dick-a-Dick caught it and everyone was happy.

His clock, though his most cherished prize, was not the only one. In the course of the tour he accumulated a vast collection of watches, rings and 'brummagem' jewellery. His ultimate extravagance was a framed oil-painting of enormous size and outstanding ugliness. Maybe this was the last straw which broke the back of his obsession; perhaps it gave him an opposite, but equally powerful, urge to get rid of his kickshaws. The watches and tie-pins were easily shed. His generosity was as large as his extravagance and he bestowed the jewels upon his comrades as though he were an Oriental potentate. But what of the picture? Nobody could wear that as a tie-pin. The resourceful Shepherd suggested that he should raffle it among the guests at their hotel for a sovereign at half a crown a time. Dick-a-Dick took a ticket himself and, as the number of entrants, including himself, stuck stubbornly at seven, he was obliged to take another, and, in support of this second claim, he rattled the dice and threw a number so large that it was obviously the favourite. For a moment he was faced with the perilous risk of winning the beastly thing himself, but was rescued by an eager competitor who offered him ten shillings for this golden chance. Dick-a-Dick promptly released the ticket which, equally promptly, won the prize, so once more he secured the greatest happiness of the greatest relevant number.

'Dick-a-Dick,' commented Shepherd, 'was perfectly satisfied,' and added in near-immortal words. 'He had no appreciation of art.'

Our Aborigines could all throw the spear and boomerang, but Charley Dumas was outstanding. He had been a champion in his own land and was undoubtedly paramount here. Great crowds came to see him hurl the slender stick almost out of sight and apparently keep it voyaging, rather like an antipodean sputnik, by remote control. Gaping, spectators would see it return, slowly and, as it seemed, deliberately, to make a perfect three-point landing between Charley's bare feet. In the last fifty years much has been learnt about the control of aircraft and missiles from the ground and the science of aerodynamics has few secrets, but much of the mystery of the boomerang remains. Some newspapers suggested that more people came to see Charley Dumas' bravura performance than to see the cricket and, although this is not strictly true, Dumas had a large following.

The master of the Australian stockwhip was Jimmy Mosquito, the brother, in spite of their different names, of Johnny Cuzens. Jimmy was demonstrably inferior to Johnny as a cricketer and a sprinter, but with the stockwhip he displayed the same touch of wizardry as did Charley Dumas with the boomerang. Between lunch and the resumption of play Shepherd introduced a pretty ritual. Outside the pavilion he would stand with a shilling in his outstretched fingers and Jimmy, with a nonchalant crack of his eighteen-foot lash, would flick the coin clear. This performance was repeated two or three times and then Shepherd would toss the shilling to Jimmy as his prize. From the knot of spectators who had gathered to watch this little game, one man after another would come forward, waving his shilling and inviting Jimmy to flick it out of his hand. By the time the bell rang for resumption of play, Jimmy's pockets were bulging with shillings. But his ethical standards remained high. After his haul he always returned his partner's decoy shilling.

The poverty of some of the visitors in cricketing skill had probably a basic cause in the state of their health, for which the English climate may be held responsible. Fine and warm as was the English summer of 1868, it was not so dry as summer, or even winter, in their own Australia; several of them suffered from chest complaints and one of them died. King Cole was taken ill during the match at Hastings and was sent up to Guy's Hospital, where he died, as Fred Grace was to die twelve years later, from congestion of the lungs. Some fragments of a rambling elegiac poem mourned him sadly and this, along with his photograph among his comrades in the museum at Lord's, are all we have to remember him by:

> *Now run out for nought in the innings of life*
> *By the grave of the good he is sleeping;*
> *Yet sad are his comrades, though reckon they well*
> *How safe is their mate in our keeping.*

A sad and sincere effort, but I do not think poor King Cole would have liked that 'run out for nought'. Though kindly meant, it seems a distressing commentary on human effort.

An odd point about the Aborigines was that on their return home, though two or three of them turned out in State cricket, none of them achieved any success. Johnny Mullagh, by far the highest of them in capacity, played happily in good club cricket, and when he died at the age of fifty he was buried in his club blazer. There is a splendour in his epitaph: 'He was a cricketer to the core.'

CHAPTER 7

Some Innocents Abroad

I

LONDON River is wide and muddy, but the Thames, when it rises, is, or should be, a clear trickle. The contemporary torrent of cricket tour books is turgid and turbulent, but even this flood must have begun somewhere. The very first of the tour books has the comfortable Victorian title, *The English Cricketers' Trip to Canada and the United States in 1859*. It was written by Fred Lillywhite and, if the present writer is a little behindhand in 'noticing' it, he must confess that it fell into his hands a little late in the day.

The Lillywhite family can be almost as puzzling to the layman as the Bach family. At best, it leaves him with the bewildered and slightly aggrieved impression that there were an awful lot of them. The first was old William (Lillywhite, of course, not Bach), 'the Nonpariel', who claimed that he bowled the best ball in England, and defined cricket at its glorious zenith as: 'Me bowling, Pilch batting and Box keeping wicket.' This William had three sons: John, who did some respectable batting for Sussex and was editor of the *Cricketer's Companion* from 1865 to 1885; James, a fair cricketer and school coach at Westminster; and Fred, who was author of this present tour book and the first man ever to produce and print score-cards on the spot. A pioneer, if ever there was one. These three lads had a cousin, another James, commonly known as Lillywhite Junior. He visited Australia with W. G. Grace's first touring team in 1872–73 and later, as a business venture, took out the side that played what is now recognized as the first of all Test matches, Bannerman's match at Melbourne in March, 1877.

But Fred is the man for our money, a one-man battalion of camp-followers, a fussy forerunner of a later age's ideal factotum, the efficient and unfussy 'Fergie', who died 'in harness' almost a hundred years later. It is impossible not to be impressed by Fred Lillywhite. In the businesslike manner of a snail, he carried his tent and printing press round the world virtually upon his back. Even when the ship was storm-battered in mid-Atlantic Fred thought more of his paraphernalia than of the safety of passengers and crew, or, to be quite fair, of himself. Amid constant perils of field and flood, Fred and his tent were always in the van, a possible inspiration and an undoubted nuisance to everyone within range. The engraved title of the work depicts the author, sitting in his tent, score-books in front of him, printing press behind him, and a look of ineffable self-satisfaction on his face. Indeed, his expression suggests that of the seaside mayor who once had a shelter erected on his town's promenade with the inscription: 'Presented by His Worship, Alderman Wiggings. *The Sea is His and He Made It.*' Fred's picture almost seems to claim that Fred invented cricket and that, at any rate, the game could not get very far without him. Authors have lost the knack of looking so imposing. It is one disillusion brought by television.

The tourists of the 1859 adventure were not merely chosen from the cream of England's professionals; they *were* the cream. Half of them were from the All England Eleven and half from their rivals, the United England Eleven. The night before they sailed they were photographed on the deck of their ship, against a background of masts, spars, rigging and bulwarks, so tightly packed together that movement must have been difficult. The photograph does not appear in the book itself, but you can see a copy of it at Lord's. The players are grouped round their captain, the handsome George Parr, who looks rather like Dr. Livingstone, a Livingstone on whose good nature no one could presume. In their polka-dotted white shirts, they look a sturdy lot, genial in outlook, except perhaps for John Jackson, who has a cricket ball in his hand and a wicked gleam in his eye, and appears to resent any delay in getting on with his normal business of being 'fearful'. Caffyn, Lockyer, H. H. Stephenson and Cæsar, who holds a bat, were Surrey men; Parr, Grundy and Jackson were from Nottinghamshire; Wisden, the 'little wonder', and John Lillywhite were from Sussex; and Diver, Hayward and Carpenter, who also holds a bat in the picture, were from the once-powerful shire of Cambridge. The players received only £50 and their expenses, so none can have made a fortune out of the trip, though none was the worse for it.

The book presents, in happy phrase, a number of original features. It contains twenty-four full-page illustrations, and, of these, only one, the frontispiece, shows any reference to a cricketer in action. (This is a lifelike portrait of the Surrey warrior Lockyer, shown keeping wicket in the absence of any batsman or bowler against a backcloth peopled by elegantly-dressed ladies and gentlemen, with Fred, complete with tent, upstage right, as if it was as much as the engraver's life was worth to leave him out of the picture.) A few of the illustrations depict life at sea in 1859, lived at horrific angles. The only consolation in all this pictorial pitching and tossing is that, however dizzy their inclination to the horizontal, the storm-harried passengers always preserve a mien of grave dignity. Most of the other pictures are 'straight' views of objects, or episodes, of interest: the game of shuffleboard, in which the officers had a slightly unsporting advantage, based on their inside knowledge of the roll of the ship; a North Atlantic iceberg of majestic proportions; a Mark Twainish river-boat, stern-wheel and all; a genuine four-horse stagecoach that might have come rumbling straight off a Hollywood Western set with Hopalong Cassidy galloping after it; several interesting shots of Niagara, with captions in verbal Technicolor; and, as though the illustrator were working up to a terrific climax, a truly rousing front elevation of the tourists' hotel in Montreal.

The record of the tour is set down, journey by journey and match by match, in leisurely fashion and full scores of all the games are given under the reassuring heading:

CORRECT SCORE
From F. Lillywhite's Printing Tent of Lord's and
Kennington Oval, London

Every incident passes before the reader's eye in minute detail, from the heaving horrors of the Atlantic, which effectually silenced poor Jemmy Grundy, 'his heart being too full for utterance, except in one peculiar way', to shuffleboard matches played on deck for champagne prizes (Moet's best at 6s. a bottle.) The heaving was genuine enough. Caffyn swore that he would not venture to leave England again, under any circumstances; 'if he did, he would forfeit £100 . . .' (Two years later he went off on the first tour of Australia, came back home and returned two years later still. This time he stayed in Australia to coach, and there is happily no record of his forfeiting £100 to anybody.)

When the weather on the voyage grew worse, Fred wrote with feeling: 'We had no concert this evening, being totally unable either to sit, stand, walk, or do anything but to bring one's self to an anchor on deck, and stand the drenching . . .'

The travellers' landward adventures were not quite so hectic, though they included a Sunday sight-seeing drive 'to view the maple trees in autumnal glory' and a match which lost its third day in a snow-storm and ended on its fourth with the tourists fielding, like Eskimo hunters, in mufflers and overcoats. There is a sombre majesty in Fred's apostrophe to Niagara, 'over which magnificent precipice the irresistible tide rushes at the rate of one hundred million tons of water every hour'. When they told this to Ephraim Lockwood on a later tour, he replied: 'I see nowt to stop it.' These two views represent the romantic and the realistic. And both of them are right.

The tourists travelled 7,364 miles and, though no batsman made anything like a big score, all the bowlers took bagfuls of wickets. In the first innings of one game, playing against odds, Wisden captured sixteen wickets for seventeen runs. You could almost have forgiven him if he had instituted a cricketer's almanac merely to perpetuate the record of such a feat. A typical match was the one at Philadelphia, a city which was, for three generations, cricket's stronghold in America. The first day was rendered blank by rain, which was normal for Englishmen, and the second by an election, which shocked them deeply. On the third day they won easily, Jackson taking fourteen wickets at some incredibly low cost.

From the beginning of the volume to the end there is never a dull moment. The first sentence reads: 'On the Evening of September 6, 1859, Twelve Cricketers of England met at the George Hotel, Liverpool, to be in readiness to embark . . .' It suggests the intriguing opening of an historical romance, which indeed it is. The only odd thing is that fifteen years after Martin

Chuzzlewit, and two years before the Civil War, the book tells you nothing about what went on in America or what Americans were like, except that, as now, they were generous and enthusiastic. Still, you cannot have everything.

The final section leads the way to glory and comprises, as you might say, a ball-by-ball description of the dinner given at Godalming to the heroic Surrey members of the returning team. The toasts numbered fifteen: the Queen, the Prince Consort, the Army and Navy, the Bishop and Clergy of the Diocese, the Lord-Lieutenant of the County, the Twelve Touring Cricketers, the Mayor and Corporation of Guildford, the Visitors, the Local Cricket Clubs, the Vice-Chairman, the Dining Committee, Fred Lillywhite (and his tent), the Press, the Scorers and Umpires, and (no doubt as a hurried afterthought) the Ladies. And every toast was drunk with three times three. Let us at least show these drinkers reverence, though emulation is beyond our power.

For me the book has one small fault, and this concerns the mournful, if oft-repeated, complaint: 'What this pitch wants is ten minutes of the heavy roller.' Our author states that this observation was made by John Wisden in 1859 on the Atlantic. Now, I have always maintained that this was what Tom Emmett said in 1876 in the Bay of Biscay. I think it no shame to confess that I have dined out on the Emmett version for years and, as a Yorkshireman, I part with it very sadly.

II

IT is only occasionally that I am privileged to enter the Long Room at Lord's and normally I am happier there than 'anywhere else on earth'. But I remember an afternoon last summer when play was passing, let us say, through a temporary period of suspended animation. Or so it seemed to me as I sat on the edge of the long quasi-refectory tables and gazed out through the pavilion's great plate-glass windows. Perhaps it was the effect of so much glass, for the mighty middle doors were closed; perhaps it was the fact that all sounds seemed deadened by the failure of the bat to hit the ball with sufficient violence. As I gazed out in front of me, the players seemed to be goldfish moving with slow, silent purposelessness in some gigantic goldfish bowl.

Now in watching cricket I feel in sympathy with the old lady who didn't like green peas. 'I'm glad I don't like green peas,' she said, 'because, if I liked them, I should eat them, and I *hate* them!' Similarly, I am glad I am never bored with cricket, because if I were, I should stop watching it, and I couldn't bear to stop watching it. I will not go so far as to say I was bored, but, until the play sailed out of the doldrums, the risk was always there; my sky was shadowed by a cloud the size of a man's hand, encased, as it might be, in some stone-waller's batting glove. My one hope was to retreat to the long restaurant behind the Long Room and have a cup of tea.

It is an excellent restaurant, providing, for the physically and spiritually parched, drinks of varied strength; for me its most fascinating feature is the long, narrow shelf that runs round the wall opposite the bar. On this you can balance your tea-cup and gaze with delight on the faded photographs of touring teams which festoon the wall from shelf to ceiling. Wherever you look they are there: history in flannels, stretching back from the carefree youngsters of to-day to the era of the demon Spofforth and of John McCarthy Blackham, whose beard was as fierce as that of Blackbeard the Pirate. Munching your bun, you can gaze still further back into the dark abysm of time.

Who, for example, are these men, photographed and taste-fully tinted in colour by a long-dead artist (rest his soul) in Bourke Street, East Melbourne? The picture was taken in January, 1862, and is an excellent example of photography for its period. It portrays twelve cricketers captained by H. H. (Heathfield Harman) Stephenson, the first team to voyage across perilous seas to Australia in the service of the game. In addition to the players, you will see three top-hatted figures. One is the manager, Mr. Mallam, who was responsible for the main arrangements and had made most of them beforehand. The other two are Messrs. Spiers and Pond. I had often heard the names of the eminent catering firm, but had never thought to catch sight of their likenesses in cricketing company. Yet here they were. If anything looked more impressive than Mr. Spiers, it was Mr. Pond, and if anything was more impressive than Mr. Pond, it was the balloon floating in the sky at the top right-hand corner of the picture, an addition which the artist had thrown in, I was convinced, to give a poetic touch to a businesslike gathering.

The English team which travelled to Australia in 1861, like the English team which played at home in 1957, was mainly built on a Surrey framework. H. H. Stephenson, their captain, was a genuine all-rounder in that he was not only a fast bowler with a devastating off break, and one of the best bats in the side, but a first-class wicket-keeper into the bargain. Among his county colleagues were such stars as William Caffyn and George Griffith and near-stars such as Charles Lawrence and Tom Sewell. Surrey's preponderance in the English twelve was not wholly due to their high quality, though that was very high indeed. The fact is that the harder-headed northern players, encouraged in their economic doubts by George Parr, could not bring themselves to accept the terms offered, which were £150 each, plus expenses; that is, just three times as much as had been received on the American tour of two years before. The Surrey club loyally stepped into the breach; and then, among those who joined the Surrey captain and his six club-mates, were Roger Iddison and another Stephenson (Ned), both of Yorkshire, and Tom Hearne of Middlesex, one of a family even more prolific in producing cricketers than the Lillywhites.

Roger Iddison, who came from Bedale, was a character more joked against than joking. He was a lob bowler so slow that he could run after the ball and fetch it back if he thought it was not going as straight as he wished. Or so Tom Emmett said. Roger clean bowled a good many eminent batsmen, more often than not through their own sheer exasperation. This happened once or twice to W.G., but, to do him justice, the Grand Old Man had usually scored a hundred or so first. Though generally a sound batsman, Roger would play forward, as though it were a religious rite, at the first ball he received and bowlers who knew this could get him out. Roger knew they knew, but he still played forward, unable to help himself. He remains, philosophically speaking, a sad example of duck-prone determinism.

The team travelled slowly and arrived at Melbourne on a broiling Christmas Eve. There is another picture at Lord's which shows the uproarious welcome given to them by the peasants and workers, as many as ten thousand of them. From the quay they were driven in triumph (and a coach drawn by six white horses) to the Café de Paris, which had the twin advantages of being fronted by Corinthian pillars and owned by Mr. Spiers. Knots of excited citizens were waving at every window, climbing every lamp-post, and pressing round the coach in carriages, carts and buggies. Not content with trying to overturn the coach in their excitement, a commando troop of enthusiasts climbed on top and sat there, swinging their legs over the coach windows and hiding the slightly bewildered faces of the visitors imprisoned inside. At last the prisoners escaped into the hotel, where they were sumptuously entertained; Mr. Spiers would see to that. The enthusiasm must have continued through the night and well into the next day, for it was almost impossible for the cricketers to get out of the hotel. Finally, they were able to slip out and hold their first practice at point X far out in the bush. Can you imagine an Australian touring side, instead of having their first practice in the Nursery at Lord's, being whisked off to a secret rendezvous somewhere on the far side of Richmond Park?

When the visitors were at last in a position to start their first match, played against Eighteen of Victoria, they turned out, to the cheers of 15,000 spectators, in a uniform even nattier than that which was to be worn by the very first Australian visitors to England seven years later. Each player, for identification purposes, wore a sash, just as the Aborigines were to do; each, too, was topped by a straw helmet, decorated with a bright band to match the sash. The most memorable thing about this match was the terrific heat, which rose to a temperature quite outside the temperate Englishman's experience; it did not, however, prevent Caffyn and Griffiths from batting far more efficiently than anybody on the other side and the English bowlers from taking their deadly toll, so that in the end the visitors won by an innings and nearly a hundred runs. As the last wicket fell, the balloon which was *not* our artist's invention, but had been coyly nestling in the corner of the ground, rose proudly wafted by 15,000 cheers, and sailed in splendour over Melbourne's skyline, trailing a banner which bore the balloon's honoured name, *The All England*.

It would be a pedestrian understatement to say that the

visitors' journey through Australia was a triumphal progress. Wherever they went, church bells rang, bands played and the local mayor commanded their presence at breakfast. Not all their matches were so successful as the first but, out of a dozen games played, they won six, drew four and lost only two. One of these defeats was at the hands of a combined Twenty-Two of New South Wales and Victoria and this was probably the only time in history that Australia was able to put her best two elevens into the field at one time and on one side. Local poets saluted them:

E is for Edwin Stephenson—not easily got out,
A Yorkshireman and, like the rest, he knows his way about.
I stands for Iddison, a cricketer all round,
And gladly will we welcome him upon our local ground.

Everybody had the time of his life. It would be difficult to recall any visitor who was not rendered happy by the tour. Caffyn, that elegant stylist, did finely with the bat, Sewell with the ball and Griffith with both; H. H. Stephenson acquired a reputation for after-dinner speaking that would have flattered Demosthenes, and if Messrs. Spiers and Pond were not solaced by a profit of £11,000, they were hard to please. Roger Iddison summed up the pleasures of Australian hospitality in a letter home: 'We are made a great fuss of; the Queen herself could not have been treated better.'

One player to show his appreciation of Australia's welcome was Charles Lawrence, who accepted a coaching post with the Albert Club of Sydney. He was by no means the first of cricket's missionaries to carry the torch to Australia's heathen land. Isolated English settlers started the game, cutting rough pitches in the bush, wherever they went. Lawrence's chief claim to fame is that, as a coach, he placed instruction on a firm basis and taught literally hundreds of young men to develop their talents. The second first-class teacher was William Caffyn, the Reigate barber and Surrey all-rounder, who had been to America in 1859 and to Australia in 1861–62. He was a member of the second team to tour Australia two years later. (You will remember his solemn vow never to cross the sea again.) One thing is fairly certain: if there had been no Lawrence and Caffyn, there would have been no Trumper and Bradman.

III

THIS second touring side was captained by the seasoned
warrior, George Parr, and Surrey was not quite so strongly
represented in it as before. Griffith was with his Surrey clubmate again and another stalwart was the Yorkshireman George
Anderson who, like Roger Iddison, came from Bedale. His
photograph looks like that of a slightly sombre Charles
Dickens, a Dickens engaged in writing *Hard Times*. His
solemn expression suggests that he may be bearing, as a burden, the sorrows of the world, but he may merely have been
suffering from stomach trouble. Cricketers are on the whole a
land-lubberly lot, but Anderson must have been a more con-
sistently seasick passenger than all the rest of them, and this
was especially hard, for he was an enthusiastic and hearty eater.
Richard Daft described him as 'a great hand at pies and
cheese cakes'. The most striking member of the team, however, was its only amateur, E. M. Grace, a tremendous fellow
then, as always. The tour was even more in the nature of a
royal progress than the previous one. Many thousands came to
watch the games in the cities and enthusiasm had reached the
boil before the first ball of the first match. This was watched
by an enormous crowd, one-third of whom were ladies. The
tourists did not lose a single match, though they had to fight
with their backs to the wall in order to secure their victory
(by one wicket only) in the game against the Twenty-Two of
New South Wales. Ten victories and six draws out of sixteen
games made a highly creditable record. Parr captained the side
with his usual forceful shrewdness, and though he was no
orator, as Brutus and H. H. Stephenson were, he piloted his
side with skill through an enjoyable tour. Cricket did not use
up all the tourists' energies and often, after a match, they
would take part in the local athletic sports. Here E. M. Grace
was in his element and his successes in running, jumping and
hurdling were immensely popular. One of the most delightful
qualities of E.M., and indeed of all the Graces, was that his
obvious zest and enjoyment were so happily conveyed and
transferred to those who played with him or watched him.

George Anderson left behind him some impressions of this
tour. The outward voyage took sixty-one stormy days and

looked like taking more, but the captain sailed on in the teeth of many a gale, inspired by one of the noblest of human ambitions: he had vowed to eat his Christmas dinner in Melbourne. And eat it he did. George Anderson may have been ready, on arrival, for the Melbourne goose, but while on board ship took no pleasure in even the thought of eating. In his berth he remained and did not dare to attend even the smoking concert in the saloon at which a fellow-passenger sang a gay topical song:

> *There's cricketers bold, the Eleven of All England,*
> *A fine set of fellows as e'er crossed the sea,*
> *I hope soon to see them with bat and ball in hand*
> *Astonishing the natives of proud Austral—ee.*

The tourists had an even bigger public reception at Melbourne than their predecessors, and practically every man who had emigrated from Yorkshire to Australia queued up outside Anderson's hotel room to slap him on the back and drink his health. There was not the slightest suggestion of cause and effect in the fact that not long afterwards, while on a possum-shooting expedition in the bush, Anderson trod on a hideous black snake about four feet long. He fled in terror back to the sheep station of his host, who had been regaling him the previous evening with horrid stories of venomous reptiles, almost going back to the old Serpent of Eden. Happily Anderson was unpunctured, if not unperturbed, and his deadly snake turned out, on inspection, to be a walking stick. He had some interesting things to say about the rewards of the tour, and reckoned that each player was (or might reasonably have been) left with about £250 clear, after paying expenses. He added one cryptic observation which poses a fascinating question mark over a vast territory of speculation.

'I might just mention,' he said, no doubt with the dead-pan expression which normally accompanies such remarks, 'that they did not expect us to abandon cricket matches to go to the races.'

And that is all he would ever say.

IV

IN 1879 Richard Daft, that handsome, graceful batsman, captain of Nottinghamshire and All England, took a team of

Notts and Yorkshire cricketers to America. The voyage, though not so utterly perilous as that of the *Nova Scotia* had been twenty years before, was choppy enough, and just to make sure Daft kept in his cabin until the mouth of the St. Lawrence was reached. His only consolation was the philosophic reflection that these matters are relative. At least he was not as sick as Barnes, who nearly died.

Of the five Yorkshiremen in Daft's team, three of them, and especially two of them, seemed to spend most of their time ragging the life out of the fourth, who was Ephraim Lockwood, 'old Mary Ann'. George Ulyett, Tom Emmett and, to a certain degree, George Pinder were gay extrovert characters, given to continuous bursts of elementary if not very edifying humour. Sometimes they would torment each other, as when somebody placed a handful of worms in one of Tom Emmett's socks which he had taken off to dangle his feet in Niagara water. For an instant he was convinced that he had found a snake, and yelled loudly. Then, when he found out who had played the trick, he yelled louder still, swearing a vengeance that he never succeeded in wreaking.

But most of the time it was easier to band together and take a rise out of old Mary Ann, who was infinitely good-natured, 'gormless' and rather slow—except when he had a bat in his hand. You have only to look at his photograph to see his expression, the sort of kindly innocence which marked him out as a natural butt. You already know his classic observation on being asked to admire the might and majesty of Niagara. The remark has been attributed to every Yorkshire tourist from that day to this. The last time I heard it, it had been handed down (and handed over) to Johnny Wardle, caught in the act of apostrophizing the Victoria Falls on the River Zambesi. Ephraim would not have minded. He only wanted to be safe home again. He was a 'poor traveller'; he 'reckoned nowt' to foreign parts. 'If that's Niagara,' quoth he solemnly, 'give me Lascelles Hall.' The only road that he recognized as a happy road was the one that led up from Huddersfield to the stone-built windswept village which rivalled Hambledon as the cradle of English cricket.

There are some innocent persons to whom 'everything' seems to happen and everything happened to Ephraim on the

American trip. When he and Pinder went out for a stroll together, for some mysterious reason he always walked a yard or two behind, but they talked to each other all the time as if they were side by side. (I have seen more than one married couple walking like this in the streets of Bradford, the husband leading by a yard and a half, but the reason is still a mystery.) One Sunday morning Ephraim and Pinder were dragged off to church and the glad news was quickly whispered round that Ephraim had come without any money in his pocket. There was quiet betting as to what he would do when the plate came round, but Ephraim beat the book. Gently he closed his eyes and slept peacefully, a reverent expression on his face, and only returned to consciousness when the plate was safely past. Most of Ephraim's colleagues were impervious to mosquito bites, but he suffered cruelly. Sometimes his innocent face was so swollen that they asked him if he had been having half an hour with Jem Mace. One morning George Pinder appeared in the hotel dining-room with cheeks heavily puffed. When his friends laughed, he muttered: 'All right, all right, wait till you see Mary Ann.' A few moments later Ephraim crept stealthily in and, in order to avoid notice, slid into an inconspicuous corner near the door. His face was so swollen as almost to hide his identity and he hoped against hope, in his tortured self-consciousness, that by this very disguise he might avoid recognition. But Pinder, who was not to be deceived, greeted him with a whoop of joy. Ephraim, if the expression may be used, had been spotted. At once the entire population of the dining-room rose from their breakfast to give him a rousing reception.

Yet, although his companions loved to pull his leg and make game both of his diffidence and his rather large, heavy boots, they acknowledged his skill at the crease and they cheered him to the echo when, though suffering from the most poisonous mosquito bites, he made 80-odd on a nasty wicket by a display of combined courage and artistry that they had seldom seen surpassed. After that, he never played a poor innings and by the end of the tour found himself almost at the top of the batting averages.

Daft writes with dignity and a certain pathos of the voyage home. It was not, he maintained, as bad as the voyage out; that is, whereas on the way out he ate nothing at all, on the way home he was able to indulge in a little gruel every day. And every day his team-mates would drop in and tell him what a perfectly splendid meal they had just enjoyed in the canteen.

V

EMBARK with me on one more tour. The year is 1879, the same year that saw Richard Daft's excursion. The players were not English, but Irish of the Irish, and their exploits are boisterously celebrated in a rare volume entitled *The Irish Cricketers in the United States 1879* by *One of Them*. Even more minutely than Fred Lillywhite's book, this deals with the personal adventures of the players, giving less and less attention to what happened on the actual field of play. There is a fascination in the opening sentence: 'There was something unusual going on at the Kingsbridge Terminus, as the American Mail lay beside the platform, awaiting its weekly burden. Here and there might be seen pieces of luggage marked with a strange device. On each was a large circular badge with letters printed in green upon it, which, on closer inspection, were seen to spell "The All Ireland Eleven". . .'

Who could resist a start like that? The book is a short one of a hundred pages and has thirty-five chapters, all with exciting headings, the first ten of them devoted to the voyage out. Of the visitors, at least four were *Hones,* all ancestors in some degree of Patrick Hone, author of the recent delightful volume, *Cricket in Ireland.* ('We had a N. Hone, a G. Hone, two W. Hones, and later on a J. Hone, but unfortunately not a single O'HONE amongst the lot.') It is difficult to assess their absolute value as cricketers, but one of the happy Hones at least had something in common with W. G. Grace. He took his bride across the sea with him and the tour was their honeymoon.

What struck the visitors most on landing at New York was the impression they gained that all the men were thin and wore long mustachios and all the horses were thin and wore long tails. It seems an odd phenomenon to be the first that observant in-comers noticed, but then, of course, the New York skyline as we prostrate ourselves before it to-day was not there to be admired in 1879. Furthermore, their first fine careless impression was modified by a second impression that there were also men with short mustachios or no mustachios at all. There were even some fat horses with short tails. The visitors, therefore, seem to have been extremely fair-minded in their observation.

They first took the field in a game against an eleven of the St. George's Club. It had been expected that they would play against odds, but the Irish captain made up his mind that, whatever happened afterwards, they must not be beaten at the first attempt. He therefore, despite the protests of some of his men that they would willingly have played against twenty, insisted on equal numbers. As things turned out, he need not have worried. The Irishmen rattled up nearly two hundred and, as for their opponents' reply, 'their first innings closed for twenty-five; their second showed an improvement of ten runs'.

In this cheerful spirit the tour proceeded, encouraged by victories over their opponents by day and relaxed by bouts of banqueting in the evenings. The narrative is not crippled by statistics and there is no serious attempt, as in Fred Lillywhite's book, to set down the scores. On the other hand, there is hardly a drink, much less a meal, that goes unrecorded. Even in 1879 American hospitality was overpowering and the author quotes a bill of fare which covers a full closely-printed page of the book and runs the full gamut of culinary ingenuity, from oysters, shrimps and Kennebec salmon, by way of beef, veal, lamb and grouse, to a huge ice pyramid on which the figures of cricketers, lions and eagles were carved, apparently roaming the slopes as though these were their native habitat. In the course of such a dinner, says the author, the pangs of hunger almost ceased to wound. Mark that down for your collection of happy understatements.

The Irish won their match at Syracuse by an innings on a pitch which had once been an old Indian war-path and was full of arrow-heads and flints. It would be a pitiful example of meiosis to admit that this wicket helped the Irish bowlers; the Syracuse batsmen merely heaved successive sighs of relief when their wickets were scattered and they could return once more to the safety of the pavilion. At Staten Island the tourists met a fiercer foe, Ephraim Lockwood's old friends, the mosquitoes. All the Irishmen were attacked, and only one, Mr. Casey, secured immunity, mainly because his beard faced the attackers with something like a barbed-wire entanglement. The home Eighteen staved off the innings defeat by one run and, in forcing the Irishmen to bat again to knock off the single, were cheered by their supporters as if they had won a famous victory. The match at Hoboken was won by a 200-run margin, but victory was delayed and only obtained on the stroke of time. So—splendid achievement—'we saved the match from a draw'.

It was at Philadelphia that the Irish met their Waterloo. In the City of Brotherly Love they had some brotherly cricket, for there they met a team containing as many Newhalls as they themselves contained Hones. There were George, Robert and Charles and the last of these added to the sharpness of his attack by his sinister passion for lemons. One of these he would keep behind the wicket and 'drew inspiration from it for each ball and each stroke'. The defeat of the visitors by this gang of Newhalls was complete and resounding. As each Irish wicket fell a carrier pigeon was sent flying from the score-box to the newspaper office in town, spreading the glad news of Philadelphia's triumphant progress. Ireland's sporting behaviour in the face of defeat received high praise in the local Press. 'Had they been victors they could not have displayed sunnier tempers or watched the fall of wickets with a gentler manner.' But the author of the book coments *sotto voce*: 'The correspondent apparently did not accompany us to the hotel, or spend the evening with us.'

To the return match, played by special arrangement the following day, there was a palpitating finish. Ireland were set 109 to win and when they had reached 107 for nine, the umpire looked at his watch and lifted off the bails. The match was over and drawn. Instantly there was a roar of disapproval from the crowd: 'Go on! Finish!' was the cry. The shouting went on until the two captains, if only to avoid bloodshed, went out on to the field and agreed to start again. The citizenry, in all brotherly love, were determined not to be baulked of a finish and the Irish knocked off the runs in one stroke amid scenes of the wildest excitement. Casey, who had made the winning hit, probably off his beard, was carried shoulder-high into the pavilion, in peril of his life. The finish, however, was nothing to the inevitable banquet, which did not break up until dawn the next day. As the author so beautifully observes, 'all did not leave at the same moment'. The dinner was superb and the decorations were carved in artistic compliment to Ireland. 'There was a melting Hibernia in ice and a harp of the same substance that wept silent tears . . .' The chairman begged that speech-makers would be merciful, but his plea went unheeded. Everybody but one man made speeches. Everybody but one man replied to everybody else. The man who did not make a speech was the one for whom the tour was a honeymoon. Towards the end of the evening, that is, about 4.30 a.m., he was called on to respond to the toast, 'the lady of the party'. The rest was silence.

He was sleeping peacefully.

CHAPTER 8

Soldiers Three

I

THERE is a certain affinity between the good cricketer and the good soldier. Both need courage and endurance; both are skilled in adapting themselves without warning to various forms of sticky wicket, as in Burma or even Bradford Park Avenue; both (though there are notable exceptions) are comparatively simple souls; both enjoy grousing about small grievances, but not about big ones; and both are prepared to play the game according to its laws, without demanding to have them altered every time some inconvenience arises.

Time has changed a good many of our notions on this theme. In 1914, and again in 1939, when we all became soldiers, our view of the soldier, as a remote person, as a character out of Kipling, changed for ever. Soldiers died for their country in tragically great numbers. So, when we were all in it together, did members of nearly every other calling. Love of country has never been a monopoly of any one lot of people. We may perhaps feel a little sceptical of a virtue, however noble, which we were ourselves forced to assume, well knowing that 'we had it not'. It is hard, nevertheless, not to feel a kind of shamefaced admiration for these pre-1914 regular soldiers; of whatever rank, who

> ... in the day when heaven was falling
> The hour when earth's foundations fled,
> Followed their mercenary calling
> And took their wages and are dead.

Going further back, we can glance at the lost world of the old peacetime soldier. We may think, judging from our own amateur soldiering, that he had a rather pleasant life, though, heaven knows, the pleasantness did not last long and will not come again. Pleasant it may have been, but it was certainly not

idle. I can think of few more strenuous lives than those lived
by some of the soldier-cricketers who played at the beginning
of the century. As a Yorkshireman, I am sorry that they nearly
always seemed to play for Hampshire, but that is not a serious
criticism. They were good men, anyhow.

Consider, for instance, Captain Edward George Wynyard.
It could be said of him, as I have said before of David Denton,
that, had he lived his cricketing life in any other period than
the springtime of the Golden Age, he might have played regularly for England. There is in existence a beautiful photograph, beautifully entitled *The Champagne of Cricket*. It was
taken in 1896 and I call your attention to the noble names it
bore:

T. Hayward, A. A. Lilley, T. Richardson, J. T. Hearne;
A. C. MacLaren, K. S. Ranjitsinhji, W. G. Grace, F. S.
Jackson, Capt. E. G. Wynyard; R. Abel, R. Peel.

This was the England side which beat the Australians at the
Oval by 66 runs. It was the only Test match against Australia
in which Captain Wynyard played, and if you want to know
how talented he was, ponder the illustrious names that bore
him company. Of the ten, I should say that only two, Tom
Richardson and J. T. Hearne, were not good for fifty runs
against any bowling. (But what superb bowlers those two
were!) Whisper the names of the others. W.G., Ranji, Archie
MacLaren, 'Jacker' . . . Of such, not to speak profanely, is the
Kingdom of Heaven. Is there one name among that shining
company that can be omitted from the muster-roll of the great?

If, on the other hand, you wish to know why Wynyard played
in only one Test match against Australia, with two on tour
against South Africa thrown in, you must remember that his
peace-time military duties, though not overwhelming, twice prevented him from accepting invitations to tour Australia. You
must also consider some of the massive names which were com-
peting for a place with his modest one: in his early days, A. E.
Stoddart, J. T. Brown, L. C. H. Palairet, C. B. Fry and Tom
Hayward; and, ten years later, A. O. Jones, F. L. Fane, K. L.
Hutchings and George Gunn. So overflowing with riches was
England's cornucopia of batting that in his finest years, say
from 1897 to 1906, he was never chosen as a Cricketer of the

Year. This omission makes one or two choices in leaner years look doubly absurd. If any further proof of his quality were needed, it could be said that in the same year as he made his one appearance against Australia, Wynyard played an innings of 268, which contained every shot in the locker. This was against Yorkshire; that is, against the bowling of Hirst, Haigh, Bobby Peel and Ted Wainwright. Need anybody say more?

He first played for Hampshire as a lad of seventeen. He came in again in the eighteen-nineties as a subaltern on leave from India and in 1893 reached an average of 50. His height and reach—he was well over six feet—made him an impressive figure at the crease. It had to be a good bowler who did not feel, at first sight of him, that there at the other end was his master. Those who saw him in his earliest days with Hampshire said that he generally wore an I Zingari cap, reinforced in polo shape. This was inclined at what was afterwards called a 'Beatty angle' and secured by a strong strap under his chin. The headgear itself was an imposing sight. Because of regimental duties, there were few seasons when he could play regularly and there were some years when he could get leave for only the odd match or two. Yet even when deprived of the bare minimum of practice, he could walk into the side at almost any time in the season and, as likely as not, score a skilful half-century.

I have already mentioned his 268 against Yorkshire, an innings which so extended the Yorkshire attack that it stretched as far as putting David Denton on to bowl, as fifth change. The same year Wynyard made centuries against Sussex (112) and against Warwickshire (111) and he topped the county's batting averages for the season.

The year 1899 might have been an outstanding one for Wynyard, had it not been for the new blaze of glory that broke from that other warrior, Major R. M. Poore. There is one glory of the moon, but a greater glory of the sun. Wynyard's average for Hampshire reached the highly creditable figure of 49.55; it just happened that the blithe new-comer, in one of cricket's most astounding spells of sustained dominance, had more than doubled it. Wynyard's centuries in that year were two: a swiftly-scored 108 against Worcestershire and a fiercely-hit 225 in an exciting game against Somerset, which Hampshire won by an innings and 150 after facing a total of well over 300 and losing four wickets for 63. Together Poore and Wynyard put on 411, a score which still remains, as well it might, a record for the sixth wicket. There was an impregnable quality about those two when batting together, though neither was in the least slow, that must have made the bowlers feel that they were trying to besiege Gibraltar by shying coconuts at the resident apes.

Twice, as we have seen, Wynyard had to decline tours to Australia—after all, he could not ask for indefinite Army leave, however much he may have deserved it—but he was able to visit South Africa twice; with P. F. Warner's side in 1905–06, when he played, though without great success, in two Tests. Four years later he made the same trip under H. D. G. Leveson-Gower's captaincy, but played in only half a dozen games. He also took part in tours to the West Indies, Egypt, America and Canada. His remotest cricketing Odyssey was to New Zealand in the English winter of 1906–07. Most unhappily he snapped a leg-tendon in the third game of the tour and so he sadly (but sensibly) sailed for home.

In Gentlemen v. Players matches he had a dozen innings between 1897–1906, the finest of which was his last in the series. At Scarborough he made 137 by splendid hooking, pulling and driving against a varied attack that contained Hirst, Rhodes, Haigh, Hubert Myers and that remarkable Northamptonshire all-rounder, G. J. Thompson. Even in Festival cricket you had to be possessed of almost unexampled dexterity to do that, especially if you were forty-five years old at the time.

It was alleged that he was a shaky starter, but the consistent heaviness of his scores shows that he was a good finisher. Like E. M. Grace, he would pull an off-ball to mid-wicket and send the next one skimming hard over cover's head. What differentiated Wynyard's pulls from E.M.'s was that the former, from his great height, would suddenly drop down on his right knee and with a raking swing lash the ball clear of mid-on's left hand. He was an especial terror to left-hand bowlers, and in his famous innings at Scarborough he was 'particularly severe' on Wilfred Rhodes, the greatest left-hand bowler in history.

His love of the game induced him to play cricket at all levels and in all parts of the world. According to his own tally, his modest boast was that he had made 150 centuries, counting Army and club games. Nor was cricket his only pastime. At the age of twenty he took part as a dashing forward on the winning side in a Football Association Cup Final, not at Wembley, not at the Crystal Palace, but at the Oval. Those were the days. At least there was something of supreme quality in a man who could win a Cup Final medal at a time when football was a really rough game and survive for fifty-five years afterwards.

II

WE can only drag Wynyard in as an eccentric because of his polo cap and his ability to slip into his county's powerful batting side and score heavily without preliminary practice, though we might give him marks for his persistence in setting out on an arduous tour at the age of forty-eight. For his friend, Major R. M. Poore, we need produce no ingeniously-turned argument. He burst upon the county cricket horizon with all the glad surprise of an artificial earth-satellite. Perhaps 'burst' is an inappropriate word for an angular-looking officer of immense height— he was six foot four and as erect as a ramrod —but his impact on cricket in the year 1899 was awe-inspiring to the point of being slightly outrageous. His outstanding capacity ought not to have provoked such surprise; he had been heard of before. While soldiering in South Africa three years previously, he had made a couple of aggressive centuries against Lord Hawke's touring team and word came back to England that this Army man was a devil of a fellow.

Home on leave in 1898, he made his first impact by scoring 50 on a fairly fiendish wicket at Lord's for the M.C.C. against Lancashire bowlers as cunning as Briggs and as fiery as Mold. In the course of his next ten games he scored two centuries: 107 against Essex and 121 not out against Derbyshire. But those who saw it give higher praise to the innings he played in his first match against Somerset. In this game he carried his bat right through Hampshire's meagre total of 97 and was undefeated at the close with 49 on the books. Here was a true and splendid gladiator, battling his way into the arena.

He was not a supremely graceful player like his contemporaries, Palairet and Spooner; they were the accepted arbiters of the elegances, but, in default of sheer grace, he had power. Few batsmen of extreme height, always excepting Frank Woolley, have appeared masters of that effortless ease which seems to waft the balls to the rails as with the flick of a silken scarf. But Poore, despite a certain stiffness in the arm, had an enormous reach and could play forward, cracking the ball to the boundary between cover and mid-off. He could, moreover, play this stroke at the sort of delivery to which most batsmen would have been obliged to play back. That extreme length of arm stood him in good stead, not merely as a batsman and slip fielder, but as a fencer, for there were few finer swordsmen in the Army of the day. At the wicket he was impatient of restraint, and above all a forcing batsman; he even forced the cautious *Wisden* into a split infinitive. 'Major Poore,' said *Wisden,* 'has a style of his own and, seeing him for the first time, it would be difficult, unless he had made a very big score, to properly gauge his merits.'

The following year there was no difficulty in gauging. Poore started the season late and, when he did so, he did not so much enter cricket as explode into it. Between 12th June and 12th August he scored 1,399 runs in twelve completed innings, with an average of 116.58. There has been nothing to compete with it, except the deeds of W.G. twenty-four years earlier, Bradman's breath-taking feats of his tours of the nineteen-thirties, and the fantastic run-getting orgies of Denis Compton's summer glory in 1947. It is a fact that nothing has ever quite equalled W.G.'s stupendous week in August, 1876, 'eight days which shook the cricket world', in which his scores were 344, 177 and 318 not out and his average, as he liked to boast, was 419.5. Major Poore did not aspire to these heights of incredibility, but he did pretty well in his soldierly way. He set off by scoring two hundreds, one of them not out, in his first game. This was against Somerset, and he followed up with another hundred (against Lancashire) in his second, so that his average after two matches was 124.3. His next score was only 11, but then he rallied with 175 and was only restricted to 39 not out in the second innings of the game because at that point he made the winning hit.

In the two Gentlemen *v.* Players games he disappointed, scoring 1, 24 and 27, but he came back into county cricket immediately afterwards in glorious fashion in the fantastic game at Taunton which we have already noted. To the partnership with Wynyard, which put on 411 for the sixth wicket, Poore's personal contribution was 304. After 36 against Warwickshire, he returned to high scoring with 122 against Worcestershire in a match in which two of the famous Fosters each made a century in each innings (W.L., 140 and 172 not out, and R.E., 134 and 101 not out). With a powerful innings of 71, Poore enabled his county to draw their game against the touring Australians. At one point the game looked like sliding in the visitors' direction, but Poore and Wynyard then came together and fought their side's way to safety. In the next game he took 79 and 53 not out from Derbyshire's excellent bowlers, and in the last game of the period he punished Leicester's attack for 157 and 32. That was the end of his season. He headed the English first-class averages with the Bradmanesque figure of 91.23 and, if you are wondering whether to assess this as a mere freak or a genuinely high figure, you should know that at the end of the same season C. B. Fry averaged 43, Jessop 33 and the magnificent MacLaren 32.

For the next three years most of England's fighting soldiers were away in South Africa. Poore came home to play in a few games in 1902 and 1904 with not very brilliant results, missed the 1905 season and then in 1906 played in two matches, averaging 58 and scoring one century as swift and severe as anything he had given to cricket seven years before. After this handsome hundred he hurt his leg and, apart from one game for a combined Army and Navy team in 1910, that was the end of his first-class cricket. He lived to fight in the 1914–18 war and to be an honour to his profession for another twenty years, attained the rank of major-general and died—he would have been professionally disappointed if he had known—just before the outbreak of the Second World War.

He had entered county cricket considerably later than most players do, and in 1899, his *annus mirabilis*, he was nearly thirty-four. At the end of that season an interviewer asked him if he could account for such success after starting to play the game seriously so late in life.

'I went through the Badminton book of cricket,' he replied, playing the question straight as he always did; 'I studied it as thoroughly as though I had had to get it up for an examination.'

Granted that a man had a character of that quality, it was a wonder that the bowlers ever got him out at all.

III

I HAVE no doubt about either the eccentricity or the high quality of my third soldier-cricketer, Hesketh Vernon Hesketh Prichard. Although in the First World War he won the D.S.O. and the Military Cross, he was not, like Wynyard and Poore, a regular soldier. He was born in India, the posthumous son of an Indian Army officer and, when less than a year old, was brought home to England by his mother, to whom he remained devoted for the whole of his life.

At school—he went to Fettes with a foundation scholarship —he showed himself to be a versatile cricketer, but cricket was only one of his keen interests. There is a lying legend that fast bowlers are creatures of limited intelligence. The whole of Prichard's life, from his schooldays onwards, was a vigorous denial of this. He was, in peace and in war, probably the most brilliant rifle-shot of his time. (He bought his first gun at the age of eleven.) While still a very young man he was an explorer of undiscovered countries and an industrious writer of travel books, of which the best known is *Where Black Rules White*, a vivid study of life in the republic of Haiti. A much more popular book, or series of books, was written in collaboration with his mother and concerned an incredibly brave, sardonic, revengeful, chivalrous, cruel and gentlemanly Spanish brigand called Don Q. This character rode through the magazines as gallantly as did his friend Conan Doyle's Brigadier Gerard at roughly the same time.

The most remarkable of Prichard's journeys was an expedition to Patagonia in search of the creature called the giant sloth, but after unbelievable adventures over rough roads, and no roads, through alternating floods and sandstorms, he came to the conclusion that the giant sloth was extinct and would never be found. Yet he had explored, almost single-handed, territories hitherto unknown. He hunted caribou in Newfoundland and elk and moose in Norway and he differed in his methods from many hunters in that he performed no act of greedy slaughter but shot only one or two magnificent specimens; for example, a stag with a head of thirty-five points.

It is easy to stress the inconsistency of a mighty hunter who is at the same time a humane man with a love for animals. Inconsistent and illogical or not, the combination can happen and with Prichard the two things went together. Outside Parliament he was the moving spirit behind a Private Member's Bill which reached the Statute Book early in 1914 and had as its object the protection of grey seals. He also worked with friends in the House of Commons to promote a Bill designed to prevent the wanton killing of birds for their plumage. This Bill had a rough passage from vested interests and faded away with the outbreak of hostilities in 1914, but after the war a new Bill was introduced and became law. Its promoters did not forget how much they owed for its eventual success to the original inspiration of a fast bowler.

It almost seemed that his early adventures were undertaken for the purpose that was to be his life's work. His high skill as a rifle-shot brought him to the notice of the Army and soon he was in France as a sniper. Within a short time he was put in charge of training for all snipers. This was the work to which he had dedicated himself and his organization was one of the most remarkable institutions in the war. During a period of leave he wrote a book, *Sniping in France*, which, despite the changes of the years, is still regarded as required reading on the complicated subject of skilled marksmanship.

His cricket had the same cavalier quality as his shooting, his hunting and his exploring. He had, of course, played any amount of school and club cricket; it was his friend Conan Doyle who brought him into the first-class game by introducing him to W. G. Grace, who was then managing the London County Club at the Crystal Palace, and to E. G. Wynyard, captain of Hampshire.

Prichard played his first match for Hampshire in 1900 and showed his quality by clean bowling L. C. H. Palairet. The next year he was too busy turning his travel notes into the book *Through the Heart of Patagonia*, but in 1902 and 1903 he came in again and captured a fair bag of wickets. These were wet seasons and in almost every way unhelpful to a tearaway fast bowler of his talents, but in the first of them he took six for 39 against Sussex, clean bowling C. B. Fry, then at the height of his sumptuous powers. In 1903 he also took seven Derbyshire wickets for 47 on a batsman's wicket. In 1904 the sun shone more kindly and this turned out to be his great year, even though Hampshire came out bottom of the county table for the third year in succession. In spite of their rich batting strength, they were a weak bowling side, but this was not Prichard's fault. During the season he took over a hundred wickets, two-thirds of them for his county, the others in representative matches of one kind or another. His best performance was not on behalf of Hampshire, but for the M.C.C. v. Kent, who were set a mere 131 runs to win, but lost by 33. So devastating was Prichard's assault that he shot down the first five wickets for four runs, three clean bowled and the other two caught behind the wicket off sharply-rising balls. For a moment it looked as if Kent were scarcely going to be able to reach double figures. After that, however, the later batsmen hit out at everything and some lusty clouts were offered, though not off Prichard. He finished the innings with an analysis of six for 23 and was reckoned to have bowled more destructively than Arthur Fielder, the England fast bowler on the other side.

The Gentlemen v. Players match of that year has its place in history for several reasons: J. H. King, the Leicestershire left-hander, who came in at the last moment for the injured Tyldesley, made a century in each innings and finished on the losing side. The Gentlemen, after being behind on the first innings (though they were not called upon to follow on) were set the task of making 412 on the last day. In the end, by the mercy of Providence and a century by Ranji that was dazzling even for him, they came to safe harbour a few minutes before time. Prichard, who was the Gentlemen's No. 10, came in at a moment critical enough to have jangled nerves of steel, but he stood firm until A. O. Jones, with a couple of resounding fours, had knocked off the runs. Prichard bowled faster than he had ever done before and it was murmured that he made the Lord's wicket look like its old lethal self of forty years before. But despite these strictures and the unfortunate fact that a very fast ball broke a bone in the back of Albert Knight's hand, Prichard bowled magnificently, the second, third and fourth wickets being flung down at the same score. King then, with a little help

here and there, made his second gigantic effort, and the attack
was blunted, but in the end Prichard had taken five wickets for
80. His victims, apart from the wounded Knight, included
Hayward, Iremonger, Denton and Arnold. He can hardly have
done more skilful sniping during the war.

Four years after the war he died of an obscure form of blood
poisoning. In one of his letters from France he had written of
courage—'the cold kind of courage, that counts the cost,
reckons up the moral obligation to proceed, and, once in, goes
on with it'. That was his own kind of courage.

CHAPTER 9

The Jokers

I

JOKES are funny things: that is, they are funny-peculiar. It is virtually impossible to demonstrate in writing that they are funny-haha. To explain that kind of joke is to kill it stone dead. I remember, with a sort of doleful satisfaction, my grim attempt to read through Bergson on *Laughter* word by word, and how, by the end, I almost reached the state of the Norman king who Never Smiled Again. The most enchanting morsels of visual comedy, as shown by Grock, or by the only greater clown, Charlie Chaplin, melt away at the touch of the typewriter. Who shall set down in words a description of Grock's immortal piano-slide or the peerless pantomime of Chaplin as, with eyes, fingers and toes, he preached his wordless sermon on David and Goliath?

I have heard a cricket crowd roar with laughter at the way Trueman pretended to throw a ball at the wicket or at Wardle's elaborate pretence of throwing up a brilliant catch when the ball was in fact speeding to the boundary. To translate that kind of laughter into words is a grim task, but it need not be undertaken grimly. There was, for instance, a hundred years ago a Nottinghamshire cricketer, Charles Brown by name, known among his team-mates as Mad Charlie. By trade he was a dyer and by temperament an insatiable enthusiast. On the cricket field he was a hard-hitting, aggressive batsman, a wicket-keeper among the best half-dozen of his kind, and a bowler of such extraordinary action that he was capable of delivering the ball from behind his back. The difference between Charlie Brown and the ordinary behind-the-back bowler, like Woolley or Wardle, is that they would swing the arm back to the front again, but Charlie could bowl and bowl straight without going to that trouble.

With this rather dastardly delivery Charlie was a menace to

batsmen. He was, however, never such a menace on the field as when working in the local dye-works. If, as he stood at his tub, someone started an argument on a cricketing theme, he would lash himself into a frenzy of excitement, violently stirring away at the liquid in his tub to underline each point in the debate. By the time the question was resolved, all Charlie's fellow-dyers had fled, for the literal purpose of saving their skins. As he stirred away with syncopated agitation, the dye flew in all directions, threatening to turn the contents of every separate vat into one glorious rainbow mixture. It was his employer's highly coloured views on this subject that turned Charlie into a full-time professional cricketer.

Billy Buttress was a ventriloquist and could manipulate his voice more adroitly than he could manipulate a bat. His batting, in fact, was deplorable and he was probably the worst batsman who ever lived, except, perhaps, J. C. Shaw. Like Dryden's Shadwell, who seldom deviated into sense, Buttress seldom deviated into run-getting. That master-mind of our day, Eric Hollies, took more wickets than he scored runs in a long and honoured career, but at least he once made 47 and was asked if he did not wish, on the strength of this tremendous performance, to rise in the batting order from No. 11 to No. 10.

'No,' said Mr. Hollies judicially, 'I prefer to keep abreast of the state of the match, so that I can regulate my play accordingly.'

Buttress never made 47, or anything like it, and his classic lament was: 'If you bowls 'em straight, I misses 'em and I'm bowled, and if you bowls 'em crooked, I hits 'em and gets caught. Either way I'm out, so what's the use?'

But give him a ball to bowl with and he was in his element; give him a long journey in a railway carriage full of country women, and he would fool them to the top of their bent. His favourite imaginary animal for introduction into this imaginary company was a kitten, hidden among the ladies' luggage and mewing pitifully. A search would begin under the seats and behind the racks; the mewing became fainter and fainter, only to rise to a shriek, as a new character was introduced into the drama. This time it was an invisible puppy, woofing good-naturedly at the kitten, and so the two non-existent creatures careered round the compartment, the dog barking and the kitten spitting and raging, until almost everyone in the compartment was driven into a state of uncontrollable agitation, all except the wicked Mr. Buttress, who lay back in his corner, like Ephraim Lockwood in church, dozing peacefully.

Sam Parr, who was a younger brother of George and an excellent cricketer, was one of the jokers who specialize in the straight face. The records tell of a knavish trick played on Tom Box, the All England Eleven's dapper stumper, whose intention had been to spend a quiet afternoon in the barber's chair. To the barber beforehand came the unconscionable Sam with the warning that he was shortly to receive a visit from a mental patient, a sad case, but harmless if tactfully handled. The poor fellow, for his health's sake, needed a very close haircut, and nothing must deprive him of it. The plot was carried out in every deplorable detail. As Tom grew suspicious, the barber spoke soothing, diplomatic words. Finally came the moment of truth, when Tom Box stood up, faced the mirror and, with dawning horror, realized that this sad, disillusioned figure in front of him, with a head like a highly polished emu's egg, was himself. He had become, though he would never live to know it, a Yul Brynner before his time.

II

A MANCHESTER man touring in South Africa was once shown that lonely grave in the Matapos hills which impresses even the most flippant and disrespectful.

'The great Rhodes,' said the guide reverently.

'What, the great Wilfred?'

'No, the great Cecil.'

'Tha'rt wrong,' said the Manchester man, 'there's nobbut one great Cecil, and his other name's Parkin.'

The first oddity about this Lancashire idol is that he was born in Yorkshire; it was only a question, he later maintained, of which end of the house, or even of the bedroom, was in which county. In the end it was decided, without recourse to the courts, that the relevant end was not in Yorkshire but in Durham, and so, Yorkshire being fussy about such things, Parkin, after one game, went off to Lancashire, who notoriously are not. He played his first game for Yorkshire and took two

wickets, having previously confessed to Lord Hawke 'the circumstances of his birth', as though these were something like a
mystery in a Wilkie Collins novel. His lordship, in jovial mood,
asked what a yard or two mattered between friends? After this
game, however, grave people began to have grave doubts about
his birth qualification and at the end of the season he departed
for League cricket where, first in Staffordshire and then in
Lancashire, he earned a rich reputation as a fast bowler, a wit
and, in the Arnold Bennett-ish sense, a 'card'.

While a schoolboy in his native town of Eaglescliffe, he had
been coached by and became the protégé of Charles Townsend,
who had given up county cricket all too soon. A dozen years
before, Townsend had been the protégé of W. G. Grace and
had played for Gloucestershire while still a Clifton schoolboy.
Nobody could have been luckier than Parkin in his first
teacher. He began his career as a fast bowler, but it was one
of his jokes to claim that his wife turned him into a slow one.
What happened was that in his eagerness to experiment with
'spin', he persuaded his wife to visit the nets and hold a bat
in front of the stumps. He confessed that he knocked her about
sadly, but apparently the lady bore this ill-treatment with
loyalty and sweet temper.

In Parkin's first game for Lancashire, in the season immediately before the first war, he signalized the entry of a spectacular new force into county cricket by taking fourteen
wickets. Owing to the way in which such matters were
arranged, he did not play a great deal more that season, but,
when the war was over, he came back into cricket as someone
to be reckoned with.

There have been some slight doubts, though I have none
myself, as to whether Parkin was a great bowler; there is no
argument whatever as to whether he was a great character. Off
the field or on, nobody could doubt it.

He had a fruitful season in 1919 and a better in 1920. I remember seeing him in the 1920 Gentlemen v. Players match at
the Oval, where he ran through a comparatively weak Gentlemen's side on a naughty wicket. Some critics at the time maintained that it was not so much good bowling as bad batting.
The same sort say the same thing nowadays if England's
bowlers do particularly well, but perhaps these critics are sub-

jected to severer temptation to be unintelligently unkind. Certainly the batsmen at the Oval that day seemed bewildered. Parkin seemed to mesmerize them. From the first ball he had them wearing that dazed expression usually exhibited by foolish members of an audience who have been dragged up on the stage by a clever conjurer to see for themselves that he had nothing up his sleeve. Parkin had everything up his sleeve. He was a genuine master of pace and length and had a colossal range of spin. He had, too, a kind of comedian's slow ball which the batsmen would step out to and miss, then step back to and miss. The victim would then pause for an appreciable moment, watching the ball as a nervous dog watches an angry cat. After that, still as earthbound as though he were shackled, he would stand stock-still while the ball bowled him round his legs. It is a trite saying, but if I had not seen it, I should have found it hard to believe. I also found it a little sad, perhaps because I tend to sympathize with the under-dog, even if my better judgment tells me that the under-dog sometimes deserves all he gets. Parkin took nine wickets and by the time he had taken four, the spectators were beginning to hoot with derision at the batsmen's efforts, so feebly frantic and so frantically feeble. It was as though the poor fellows were trying to play him on skates with an umbrella instead of a bat. None of them knew that this was Cecil Parkin's very first day in London and that he meant to make the most of it. On arriving at Euston early that morning he had seen a placard, PARKIN ARRIVES IN TOWN, which possibly had something to do with a confectioner's advertisement. That evening, with those nine wickets 'in his belt', he was sent for by half a dozen West End restaurants with a request to sample their fare. Parkin had arrived indeed.

Parkin, like any other bowler, loved to get wickets; but, perhaps even more, he loved to bamboozle the batsman, to make him look a fool, and this, though excellent tactics, was not necessarily good strategy, because most really tip-top batsmen, unlike my 1920 Oval Gentlemen, would categorically refuse to be bamboozled. But, unless faced by a batsman of the highest quality, Parkin got away with it every time. And he sometimes caught the biggest fish, too.

This sort of success won him a place in Douglas's Australian tour of 1920–21 and, in that disastrous expedition, he proved himself as a bowler to be by far the most resourceful of a not very successful lot. It was from this tour that many of the famous Parkin stories emerge. After a dire passage through the Bay of Biscay, somebody asked him if he were seasick.

'We were all seasick,' said he, 'all except old George.' (George was a notoriously parsimonious character, and, of course, his name was not George.) 'Not George, he was too blooming mean to part with anything.'

Once the Bay of Biscay was passed, Parkin became the life and soul of the ship, partly because of his conjuring tricks at concerts and partly because of his willingness to have his leg pulled. They told him that there was a fire in the stokehold (without informing him that the ship would not go without it); that a monsoon would lift the ship out of the water and balance it like a celluloid balloon on a water spray at the fair; that he would feel the bump when they crossed the Line; and that he must keep his cabin-porthole closed all the way through the Red Sea, for fear flying fishes should glide in and attack him.

Whether Parkin was in reality as big a muggins as he pretended to be, nobody will ever know. His conjuring, like that of many more professional performers, went on behind a smoke-screen of patter. His favourite trick was to borrow a florin from an innocent member of the audience and place it under an upturned glass.

'Now, sir,' Parkin would inquire, 'is your money at the top or the bottom of the glass?' It did not matter much which reply was given, because Parkin would invariably say: 'Ah, I see you know the trick,' and give the victim back his money. What the innocent did not realize as he slipped the coin into his pocket was that Parkin had 'palmed' a penny instead of the original florin. The only person to unmask this villainy was the wife of one of the Australian State Governors.

'No, Mr. Parkin,' she objected, 'I gave you a two-shilling piece.'

'Beg pardon, ma'am,' apologized the conjurer. 'I should have known. No pockets.'

J. W. H. T. Douglas was a strong and determined character and a fast-medium bowler of sharp penetration, but on this Australian tour fortune was against him, however hard—and however long—he bowled.

'That's right, Mr. Douglas,' Parkin would say, 'you go on and bowl 'em in and I'll go on after tea and bowl 'em out.'

Or, with an innocent glance at the huge, informative Australian scoreboard: 'Try the other end, Mr. Douglas, you can see your analysis from there.'

Parkin's bowling figures in the five disastrous Tests of the tour were 16 wickets at over 40 runs each and, though this was hardly a glorious feat, it was much less inglorious than anyone else's and it helped him to find a place in four of England's Test sides of 1921. Australia won the first three games right off the reel, but in the fourth, at Old Trafford, Parkin put up practically the only creditable English bowling performance of the series, and if 'Horseshoe' Collins had not stayed just under six hours for 40, until he had almost become part of the natural landscape, England might have won. It was during this Methuselah-like effort that a spectator in his agony called out to England's captain in the field: 'Hey, Tennyson, read him some of thi Grandad's poems.' And Parkin called back: 'He *has* done. The beggar's been asleep for hours!'

As it was, Parkin had taken five wickets for 38 and gained the undoubted respect of the toughest Australian side ever to reach these shores. A ploy which delighted Parkin even more was his captain's request that he (Parkin) should go in first in England's second innings, Australia having taken the sting out of the follow-on and all risk having departed from the game. Up to that point Wilfred Rhodes was the only player who had opened both England's bowling and batting against the Australians. Now there were two. Parkin went in and batted brightly for 20-odd to the great delight of the Old Trafford crowd. For a long time after that, Parkin prefaced his contributions to any serious conversation with the deathless words: 'Me and Wilfred . . .' Everyone liked Parkin and no one had the heart to spoil his story by telling him that 'me and Wilfred' were not alone. Among those who also opened England's batting and bowling were Barlow, Ulyett, Alfred Shaw, Lohmann, C. T. Studd, Jessop and (if you will believe me) Sir Jack Hobbs. But it was a good story, anyway.

Parkin was a card, and he knew it. As his bowling talents were unchallengeable, he believed himself entitled to a jester's licence in the field or at the crease. As a fieldsman he was the first to employ the trick of picking up the ball on his boot-toe and conveying it to his hands. He was also the only begetter of those tricks that Wardle perfected later: the dazzling slip-catch, brilliantly taken and warmly cheered, before spectators noticed that the actual ball had sped to the boundary; or its opposite number, the ball which everybody thought had flown to the rails, but which was suddenly, as though absent-mindedly, produced from behind the fieldsman's back. When this happened, many a batsman on his reluctant way back to the pavilion would glare at Parkin, and Parkin would smile back in friendly innocence.

As a tail-end batsman, Parkin would alternate between colossal swipes to leg from balls wide on the off with elegant forward strokes executed in the classic manner; and he would display something akin to genius in scoring runs with a ludicrously bad stroke and missing the ball completely when he had gone through the motions of a good one. Five minutes of this clowning would have the spectators convulsed and the bowlers helpless. They simply could not hit his wicket. When Parkin had had enough of it, he would proceed to run himself out. My special memory of him is seeing him running the second and third of three runs, at full speed and in simulated panic, towards the same end as his partner. Before he achieved his final departure, he would give such an exhibition of crazy calling and ribald running between wickets that spectators would have rolled in the aisles if there had been any. He had one common drawback of the comedian; he occasionally played the fool a little too hard and a good deal too long. But while his fooling was fresh, it was very, very funny.

His mirth-making habits seldom interfered with his real abilities and he did his county much service. Like the great Sydney Barnes before him, he was not always on the best of terms with the county authorities. He got into hot water over some impertinent observation in a ghosted article and was too loyal to give the 'ghost' away, even though the ghost had let him down. He was also the comparatively innocent cause of Lord Hawke's historic and mercilessly misquoted prayer about professional captains. This, with one or two other disagreements, brought his county career sadly to an end and he returned to League cricket to continue his boisterous fun for another ten years. There was in him a strain of humorous cantankerousness which militated against easy relationship, but this did not prevent him from doing great things for Lancashire. He seemed, in fact, the typical Lancashire man, the true Al Read character, even though he had been born a yard or two inside the borders of Durham. An old Lancashire player once gave me his opinion that a strong no-nonsense captain like 'Monkey' Hornby or MacLaren, might have given Parkin the benefit of an occasional friendly word (or a gentle kick in the pants) and that that would have redounded to Parkin's and everybody else's good. But he never had that good fortune and was very much the victim of enterprising journalists whose ambition was to feature him as cricket's 'stormy petrel'. But he was no stormy petrel, only a magnificent bowler and a wryly humorous character.

Cecil Parkin died in the middle of the Second World War and his ashes were scattered on the pitch at Old Trafford. This ceremony was carried out with dignity and deep feeling and with the sort of kindliness and essential decency which Englishmen will show on such an occasion. But Cecil had been a man devoid of solemnity. He would naughtily have seen a funny side in that serious moment. You can almost hear a ghostly voice murmur: 'Scatter me at the Stretford end, lads; I could always find a spot from there...'

It is sad, for more reasons than one, that Parkin is not playing to-day. He would have delighted in being the first rock 'n' roll cricketer.

III

AT the height of the unlamented bodyline controversy Patsy Hendren, of Middlesex and England, strode out to face the bowling wearing a motor-cyclist's crash helmet and, instantly on the sight of him, whatever animosity there had been in the game melted away on a gale of laughter. The crowd and the players, both friend and foe, always laughed at Patsy, though when he had scored a couple of hundred runs, many of them four and six at a time, by positively immoral hooking and pulling, bowlers must have wondered if it were all quite so funny.

Patsy, in his playing days, was a fine cricketer, a very fine cricketer indeed, but it is characteristic of him that his jokes were the jokes of a No. 11 who goes to the crease for a bit of fun, rather than of a splendid England batsman going in at No. 4. How much Irish blood runs in Patsy's veins I do not know, but his very first bubble must have been the bubble of Cockney wit and, if you meet him to-day at the foot of the score-box steps at Lord's, he will be bubbling just the same as ever, just as gaily as when he sold score-cards on the same ground over fifty years ago. No doubt in a longish life he has had his darker pains and burdens like the rest of us—toothache, seasickness, humiliating thoughts of human inadequacy and dreadful forebodings of the end of the world—but you would never think so to see his smile. Neville Cardus has gloriously observed that umpires might well at any time have given Hendren out smile-before-wicket. Half-puckish, half-angelic, that smile could bring heart to the supporters of a badly-shaken side; it was a badge of courage, a gonfalon in the thick of the combat, a Nelson's signal, calling to duty, but especially to cheerful duty. To this day it can, when curling mischievously round some mischievous reminiscence, set the table in a roar. The next happiest experience to having seen Hendren score a century is to hear him recount the extraordinary adventures of his Australian and West Indian tours. He is the perfect story-teller, humorous, sympathetic towards the victim (unless the victim, as so often, is himself), full of a sort of combined mischief and goodwill that is rarely found in humankind.

I do not believe that men have descended from apes, except in the sad sense that some of them have descended a long way. In this matter I am on the side of the angels, if only because I am convinced that they will come in again. The ape theory alone will account for neither a Schweitzer at one end nor a Hitler at the other, for mankind's occasional nobility and frequent vileness. Yet if we could imagine some touch of fairly innocent monkey-mischief in the human race, then I would not deny that Patsy has his share of it. It carries no hint of the sardonic as in the sharper humours of Parkin; Patsy has always been the happy fun-maker where Cecil could be a mordant wit.

But Patsy's humour stresses human fallibility and the comic inevitability of misfortune for the individual that makes up half of life. Sometimes it is the quick riposte, almost a reflex action. Sprinting along the boundary at Sydney Oval,

Patsy slightly misjudged and failed to hold an awkward catch.

'Garn,' cried the inevitable voice from the Hill, 'I could have caught that in my mouth.'

'So could I,' said Patsy, 'if I had a mouth as big as yours.'

Fielding in the same place, Patsy was asked: 'Why didn't they bring So-and-So out with this team?'

'Because,' said Patsy, 'they were only bringing good-looking chaps on this trip.'

'Then,' demanded the tormentor remorselessly, 'how the hell did *you* get picked?'

That would have floored a lesser man, but not Patsy, 'Ah,' he muttered darkly, 'you should see my brother.'

There is a charm about any tale of his misadventures, if only told by himself. In the backblocks of Australia he once allowed himself to be conscripted to play for a local side. Country grounds in Queensland are seldom to be found on the level, and the good-natured Patsy spent a hot and drowsy afternoon fielding on the lower side of a ridge which completely hid the rest of the field from his view. For hours nothing happened and it seemed that nothing would ever happen. Then suddenly to his sleepy eye there appeared a ball, high against the sky, soaring towards him. He ran swiftly forward and upward—he was, you will remember, a near-international soccer-winger— and breasting the slope took a miraculous catch, at full stretch, almost off his toe. It was a catch worthy to rank with the historic catches of Fred Grace and George Ulyett.

'A lovely catch, though I say it,' recalls Patsy. 'Only one thing against it: I'd caught my own captain.'

When he tells of his West Indian exploits, it is a comedy and a calypso. Only the music of the steel band is missing. In the comedy Patsy plays every part, speaking first as his puckish self and then as the West Indian heroes with their soft, endearing voices.

'So this chap Griff was bowling, a big chap, very fast, but apt to get a bit aerated. I was getting quite a packet of runs'—so far as I can gather, Patsy made 223 that day—'and Griff didn't like the way I was popping 'em both sides of the slips. So he says to old Joe, who was fielding there, "Move over a bit, Joe," but Joe says no. "Move over," says Griff, very indignant. "No," says Joe, "I don't have to do what you say, Mr. Griff, 'cause I'm an amateur and youse only a professional." "Move over, move over," says Griff. "No," says Joe, "this is the right place to stand for this slip, isn't it, Mr. Hendren?"

' "That's right," says I, dead serious.

' "There you are, Griff," says Joe, "what did I tell you?" '

This is pure essence of Patsy.

His professional talents were high, his worth to his county and his country was immense, his scores were colossal. He is the third in the list of batsmen who have scored over 50,000 runs in first-class cricket; only Hobbs and Woolley have surpassed Hendren's 57,610. Only Hobbs's 197 centuries have surpassed his 170. He was an honoured No. 5 in an England batting order that ran Hobbs, Sutcliffe, Hammond, D. R. Jardine. And after this regal line, this coronation procession, Patsy could come in and remind the world that, after all that majesty, kings could be human and cricket could still be fun.

On that conquering tour in Australia of 1928–29, under Percy Chapman's gay, youthful leadership, there was one Test, the third, at Melbourne, in which England's conquering march was temporarily halted. In this game Herbert Sutcliffe stood in the breach and played an innings even more rocklike, more impregnable than he had played at the Oval two and a half years before. Eventual victory in that match was only won by toil and sweat—by Sutcliffe's blood and England's tears.

The evening before the last day England had been set 332 to get to win and, on a wicket like the bottom of a quarry, Hobbs and Sutcliffe had fought for their country with all their skill and courage. Hobbs was out for 49, but Sutcliffe remained and Jardine stayed with him. The situation was by no means hopeless, but it was dangerous. It was tense, it was keyed up, it almost looked as though it might get out of hand.

In the dressing-room the Englishmen changed silently. The oppressiveness of the drama was upon them. Through a wonderful stand by cricket's greatest opening pair, they had staved off defeat so far, but what of the weather, what of the morrow? Patsy watched his companions as, still oppressed by nervous tension, they made for the pavilion exit. Could these be his gay *camerados*? Could these be Chapman's men? Suddenly and wildly, Patsy waved his arms. Passing the gate of the ground was a big brewer's dray drawn by a pair of horses of massive proportions and into this vehicle Patsy bundled his disconsolate companions, tall men, short men, professionals and amateurs alike. There they sat, amid crates full and empty, first dazed, then relaxed and finally uplifted. And there, with Patsy as conductor, they went bowling through the evening streets of Melbourne, singing anti-temperance songs. In the morning Sutcliffe went on to make his greatest Test century and England won by three wickets.

A little more than five years later, Hendren played in the Test at Lord's which will for ever be known as Verity's match. This was the game in which England, aided by good fortune rare at that period, won the toss, and, mainly through the high courage of Leyland and Ames, retrieved a shocking start and piled up the creditable score of 440. By the end of the second day Australia had countered with an even more creditable start of just under 200 for two. After that the deluge. On a wicket that grew stickier as the third day proceeded, Verity routed the foe twice, taking fifteen wickets for 104, the finest feat of Test bowling against Australia B.L. (before Laker). When Tim Wall, the last Australian batsman, arrived at the wicket, Hendren was standing indecently near at silly mid-on. Coming a step even nearer, he pointed to a spot conveniently in the middle of his chest.

'Place it just there, Tim,' said Patsy gently, as though suggesting that reasonable men might as well be accurate about these things.

'Go away,' ordered Mr. Wall, or its more vigorous equivalent in Australian.

But when he had hit a single and reached the other end, there again was Patsy smiling benignly.

'Put it just there,' he repeated.

It was Verity's slower and most deceptive ball and Wall lashed at it with a fury that demanded a six at least. Just as the ball appeared to pass over Hendren's head, he leaped in the air and caught it. As he did so, he turned a backward somersault and came up again holding the ball, like a native boy at Madeira, diving for pennies. He then turned three additional cartwheels in pure exuberance. England had won and the crowd were surging wildly towards the pavilion. Hendren and Wall walked in together.

'You devil!' cried Mr. Wall, but soundlessly amid the tumult.

'That's right,' said Mr. Hendren. 'Always saves a lot of trouble if you do what I tell you.'

IV

A LITTLE instruction is now necessary in the gentle art of Wardling. I once dreamed about Johnny Wardle, and oddly enough, I dreamed that I was attending that good man's funeral. This need cause Mr. Wardle no undue anxiety. It was only a dream and I will wager my golden crown (or asbestos billycock, as the case may be) that he will live at least another half-century and hit a good many more. It was an affecting ceremony and the vicar, a good, kindly man, but technically a little out of his depth, proceeded to pay a moving tribute.

'And now,' he intoned, rising to his peroration, 'we must mingle our sorrow with rejoicing. We must think of our Johnny . . . bowling away . . . under a cloudless sky . . . in eternal sunshine . . . on a perfect wicket . . . for ever and ever . . .' And Freddie Trueman, sitting beside me, tears streaming down his face, sobbed: 'By gow, that'll kill Johnny.'

There have been light-hearted cricketers before, and, oddly enough, in Yorkshire, too, but rarely has any player stepped on to the turf who can so instantly banish the encircling gloom as Johnny Wardle. He does not have to sing: *Begone, dull care!* From the moment he steps jauntily through the pavilion gateway, dull care is away with its tail between its legs. As a bowler he is bland, invitingly deceptive, and as full of tricks as a battalion of lorry-borne monkeys. As a fieldsman he has the darting movements of a blob of quicksilver, and as a batsman he is capable of waking up the sleepiest spectator who ever dozed off on a wooden bench after lunch. Merely to see him swing a bat is to feel that, dark and doubtful as the future of the human race may be, we might as well watch a Wardle innings before the worst happens.

What is it that makes such a cheerful cricketer? What, for that matter, makes a cricketer? First, I think, the single-hearted determination to *be* a cricketer. Never in the last quarter of a century has Johnny had any doubts. From the moment when he first played in the back lane with the local council's tar barrel for a wicket, a priceless (but spliceless) bat and a composition ball, he had no other thought in his head than to play cricket (eventually for Yorkshire) all summer and football (perhaps for Sheffield Wednesday) all winter. At home he hung around his village cricket ground in the hope of receiving twopence for 'putting up the tins', and in the almost incredible faith that some enchanted evening a member of a visiting side might fall sick—or drop dead—and let him, Johnny, in as a substitute. When his chance came, he seized it, literally, with both hands, so that his first treasured press-cutting read:

Schoolboy's Brilliant Catch

When he won a scholarship to his grammar school he regarded the feat with humorous astonishment until he realized that all his young friends were humorously astonished, too. This was one of the first sad facts he learned about human nature, a thing no bowler, and particularly no slow bowler, can ever know enough about. He loitered with intent about the school nets, just as he had hung about the village scoreboard, looking like the Victorian picture, 'Love Locked Out'. Hard as he tried, and well as he played at school, the first-eleven cap eluded him. (Brian Close, you remember, received his England cap before his Yorkshire one.) Wardle did better. He had won more than twenty England caps before, at an Old Boys' dinner, he was formally presented with the symbol of the School First Eleven. The delay was far too long. It is a mercy that Johnny had never heard of Freud at the time, or this continuous frustration might have had the sort of harrowing effect on him that makes meat and drink for the psychiatrists. As it was, he smiled at the thing, as he has smiled at all his other minor misfortunes.

His honours, including twenty-five England caps, have been many, but every one has been solidly and conscientiously worked for. As a player in league, county and international matches, at home and abroad, he has had to fight, though he has always fought cheerfully, for every wicket, and, even if he usually gets them six at a time, for every run. The basic fact about Wardle (J.H.) is that, though he enjoys laughter and has spread more of it around than any other cricketer now playing, he is first and foremost a 'heart and soul' cricketer, throwing every ounce of battling effort into the game for his side.

Wardle is not a clown, in the sense of the word often glibly used, meaning a fellow who does anything for a cheap laugh and plays the fool in season and out of season. When Keith Miller hit him painfully on the thigh he rubbed his elbow and when the next ball hit him on the elbow he rubbed his thigh. You will see him take a brilliant catch, slip the ball into his pocket, and pretend to rush off to save an imaginary four; alternatively he will, amid cheers, fling a non-existent catch into the air, while the real ball is speeding far away to the rails. A previous generation had seen Parkin do exactly the same thing; the present generation saw these tricks for the first time from Wardle and, foolish or not, they have given pleasure or relieved tension.

Once, after Johnny had 'wheeled away' the whole of one day under a broiling sun, I saw him send down his last over, bent and tottering, almost on his knees. It was a brilliantly impromptu thumbnail sketch of an old, old man, worn out by a lifetime's toil. Once, too, I saw him batting out an over against Ian Johnson, the Australian captain of 1956, in which the batsman carefully blocked the first five balls, an act of rare self-denial on Johnny's part. The sixth ball came down widish on the off; Johnny decided that he could not quite reach it; he therefore took a colossal leg swing at an imaginary ball on the other side of the wicket. Ridiculous? Of course it was ridiculous. But I have never heard so many people laugh so loudly at *anything*.

Wardle has the quick imagination of the perfect panto-mimist who can instantly translate a small verbal joke into an uproarious visual one. The spectators keep their eyes glued to his every movement, lest they should miss something ex-quisitely funny. His thought is as quick as his swing for six. I remember sitting next to him during a dinner at which a dis-tinguished speaker was telling the charming story of old Alfred Shaw, the Notts slow bowler, whose dying wish was that he should be buried the length of a cricket pitch away from his old friend, Arthur Shrewsbury. The request was granted, but some months afterwards some inquisitive busybody measured the distance and found it to be, not twenty-two, but twenty-seven yards. 'That's all right,' the county secretary explained, 'Alfred always took a five-yard run.'

Instantly Johnny leaned over to me and whispered: 'Five-yard run, eh? If it was Freddie Trueman, they wouldn't get him in Kensal Green!'

Johnny was by far England's most successful bowler on the M.C.C.'s 1956–57 tour of South Africa, but that was not his first visit. On a coaching engagement a few years before he found himself playing in a local league match, bowling in his own peculiar way to a packed off-side field. Three times the batsman hit the ball to cover and three times the fieldsman let it go between his legs.

Johnny appealed to his captain: 'Couldn't we,' he requested politely, 'ask the gentleman to put his legs together?'

'Oh no,' said the skipper, 'we mustn't offend him. He's the local scoutmaster.'

'Then,' cried Johnny, 'send for Baden-Powell. At least that'll make him stand to attention!'

Earnest purveyor of laughter though he is, Johnny has never let his fun interfere with his game. Laughing cavalier he may be, but, never forget, the cavalier is a fighter first and a joker afterwards. And if Wardle claims to have delivered more maidens than King Arthur and all his knights, you can reckon that the batsmen have found him pretty hard to play.

CHAPTER 10

Genial Giant

I

EVERY generation of cricketers throws up at least one who captures the imagination, not perhaps as a supreme performer, but as a boisterous personality, a mighty hitter, or both. Such a character to-day, as we have seen, is Wardle. Between wars there was C. I. J. (Big Jim) Smith of Middlesex, who now presides benignly over a pub in Lancashire. Back in the eighteen-eighties there was George John Bonnor, whose giant frame and colossal hitting powers set the crowds alight with joyous excitement all over Australia and England. Born at Bathurst in New South Wales, Bonnor came of solid Yorkshire stock. His mother, Sarah Ann Bonnor (*née* Holmes), was a lady of warm and happy personality, a member of a Yorkshire family who farmed extensively in the Gisburn district. She was born and wed in the same years as Queen Victoria and, with her husband, emigrated early in their married life to Australia. There the young couple had a more than usually difficult start, because their herd of pedigree cattle, which they had sent out in advance, was stolen by bushrangers. But the young farmer was a hard worker and a hard fighter and, after a while, he and his bride grew prosperous.

George Bonnor, who was born in 1855, was reckoned among the handsomest men of his time; a time, you understand, when there *were* handsome men, when individual features were permissible, and we had not yet developed the universal conventional male face, bald on top, fronted by thick-lensed National Health spectacles, and wearing an expression at once pompous and depressed. Bonnor's admirers said that he was six feet six in height and even his detractors allowed him six feet four and a half. Despite his enormous height, his proportions were so near to perfection that he was incapable of a clumsy movement. For so big a man, he was as active as a cat and a remarkable sprinter.

Ruskin, with less originality than you might have expected from a master of English prose, called Bonnor 'a young god', while E. V. Lucas, writing long years afterwards, lovingly recalled 'the mighty Bonnor, immensely tall, with golden hair and beard . . . this superb figure, like a god from another planet . . .' Gods from other planets, as portrayed in present-day science fiction, usually look like ambulating petrol pumps, but Bonnor was a genuine Olympian. He was not merely a god, but a sight for the gods. An English peer who visited him in Australia said that he was the most perfect physical specimen of humanity he had ever known. Not that peers are necessarily experts on standards of physical beauty, but this one was in a better position than most to know what he was talking about because, when his lordship paid him his historic visit, Bonnor was in his bath.

As a youth Bonnor played in turn for New South Wales and Victoria and came to England with Australian teams five times, all in the eighteen-eighties. His reputation as a hitter was, like the hitting itself, high, wide and handsome, and it preceded him to our shores, for the Australian temperament seldom cripples itself with understatement. The stories that English people heard were incredible but true. At Melbourne he had once driven a ball through the face of the pavilion clock. Psychologists will no doubt think up some reasons, disgraceful to all concerned, for the big hitters' weakness for hitting pavilion clocks. C. I. Thornton frequently did it and Jessop must have practically kept the clock-repairing industry in full employment for years. Even so essentially friendly a character as Sir Jack Hobbs once drove a ball straight through the clock-face at Bradford. ('Nay, Jack,' said Alonzo Drake, the afflicted bowler, 'if you'd only knocked the flamin' clock on to half-past six, we'd have been finished with this mucking about for t'day.') Bonnor, however, when he smashed his clock, bore no malice. In fact, the story that reached England was that he had sent the next ball out of the ground to a distance from the pitch, as measured by his admirers, of 164 yards.

Bonnor's renown for spectacular throwing at the wicket stood almost as high. On his first voyage to England in 1880 he bet a fellow-passenger £100 that he could throw a cricket ball 120 yards. His opponent claimed that this could not be done and that Bonnor's limit would be at least five yards less. The moment the ship reached Portsmouth Bonnor flung his cricket ball with insolent ease—practically from the gangway—over the first length of green sward in sight and was £100 to the good from that moment.

In the visiting side's first practice on Mitcham Green he took a careless swing and hit a ball 147 yards. The report of this stroke echoed round the country. On every ground that he visited spectators waited for him, cheered him wildly when he appeared and were bitterly disappointed, as though he had deliberately deceived them, when he failed. For him a tour of our country became a royal progress of violence. He used a bat weighing just under two and a half pounds and he swung it like Cœur de Lion's battle-axe.

An old and honoured acquaintance of mine, Alderman J. E. Tolson, of Dewsbury, was nine years old at the time of Bonnor's first visit. Outside the Dewsbury ground was a large private house, built by a local mill-owner, who was wildly enthusiastic about cricket. He used to dream about an imaginary six-hit which cleared the fence, the intervening road and his garden and, with an exhilarating crash, smashed the glass in his conservatory. This vision haunted the mill-owner to such a degree that he offered to stand a supper to both teams playing in any match in which such a hit was made from the middle of the ground.

On the first morning of the game Bonnor strode out, bat in hand, to have a practice knock with Alec Bannerman and it was from a dolly ball pitched up by Alec that Bonnor made his hit. It was not a tremendous skier, but went with lowish trajectory straight over the fence. This happened seventy-seven years ago, but Mr. Tolson, whose memory is youthful and vivid, says that the crash and tinkle of the glass is audible to him to this day whenever he thinks about it. I do not think that the supper took place, because the hit was not made in a match. It was not even made from the middle of the pitch, but from fifteen to twenty yards on the 'wrong' side of it . . .

Another feat of Bonnor's in Yorkshire was to throw a cricket ball from the old Lockwood ground right over the great viaduct of the Huddersfield–Spen railway. It was the highest throw that even he ever made.

In matches on this first tour Bonnor missed the ball oftener than he hit it, but in 1882 he began to make closer contacts. When he visited Yorkshire again, Bradford had the honour of seeing his first fireworks. In the second innings of the game he made only 35, but in this small total there were five sixes: one over the pavilion, one over the stand, and three to various points of the roadway, well outside the ground. You will remember, of course, that in those days sixes were not handed out for lifting a ball over a 75-yard line. Out of the field, clear of the premises, it had to go.

When Bonnor came to Trent Bridge he lofted a ball from Alfred Shaw clean as a whistle over 'Parr's tree' and out across the road—even Alletson thirty years later never did anything approaching this—and at the Oval, a big ground by any standards, he laid about him in such a manner as set the old Surrey cronies arguing whether he could hit a ball even harder than C. I. Thornton's famous drive over the old racquets courts. At Scarborough, Thornton's favourite ground, where he had once made an even bigger hit, Bonnor played against I Zingari and scored 122 out of 167, including 20 off one four-ball over: 6, 4, 4, 6. Even so short an over was too long for the bowler, who must have felt he had been struck by a hurricane. At Portsmouth Bonnor drove a ball straight over the bowler's head with such elemental force and low trajectory that it splintered the sight-screen. A stroke of that kind was no mere lucky swipe. It was controlled power. W. G. Grace reckoned that Bonnor could straight drive farther than any batsman of his time.

Bonnor was by nature a friendly soul, with malice towards none. With his happy nature, he bore no ill-will towards any person or object, except a small red ball. Like many another giant, he was shy in the presence of women, but warmly approved of by dogs and children. He would take his turn at ship's concerts or pavilion sing-songs and when he 'rendered' in his pleasant tenor voice 'The Tear in Every Eye' he quivered with honest emotion, all six foot six of him. He had another trait in common with many a famous man: he longed to be famous for something else. Your comedian secretly sees himself as Hamlet and Bonnor cherished the ambition to be known not as a slogger, but as a stylist. It is one of the sad things in life that such dreams are misunderstood and his attempts to acquire elegance filled his colleagues not with sympathy, but with rage. What, they demanded, had got into Bon? Who did he think he was? His sacred mission was to massacre the bowling, not to prance around like a dancing master.

He was gifted with a bright eye, a merry humour and a more equable temper than is usually found in a non-smoker; even when he growled, he growled good-naturedly, like a kindly bulldog. When he raced through that astonishing 122 not out at Scarborough he shared a partnership with Alec Bannerman, the Australian stonewaller whose motions while batting were scarcely visible to the naked eye. In running between the wickets there was less than perfect understanding between them.

'Catch me going in first with Lord Alec again!' cried Bonnor. 'First it's "Come on, Bon, are you asleep?" Then "Go back, you fool!" And when you've done everything he's called for, he'll come half-way down the pitch to read the Riot Act at you!'

I suspect that Bannerman, in his sardonic Australian way, enjoyed pulling the leg of an impregnably good-tempered partner.

Bonnor's hitting caused him frequently to be caught on the boundary. It was the inevitable penalty of imperial enterprise. Such sensational hitting merited and, unhappily for the hitter, provoked sensational catches. The very outrageousness of his onslaught inspired fieldsmen everywhere to do more than their utmost and he may have felt a tart satisfaction in knowing that at least three of his dismissals became landmarks in fielding history. His first big score in London—74 against the Gentlemen of England at the Oval—was brought to an end by A. P. Lucas with a dazzling catch described as 'the finest ever seen'. The most desperate catch ever taken by a Yorkshireman was a ball returned by Bonnor to George (Happy Jack) Ulyett in the Lord's Test of 1884. With all his giant strength Bonnor hammered it murderously back at the bowler. Happy Jack shot out a hand. There was a crack that echoed round the ground like a pistol shot and, by some miracle, the ball stuck. Ulyett said afterwards that it came back at him as if it had been attached to elastic. *Punch* with plantigrade humour suggested that he should be specially engaged by the Army to catch enemy cannon balls and hurl them back. The oldest M.C.C. member called him up, handed him a sovereign and told him that it was the catch of his (the oldest member's) lifetime. W. G. Grace, whose opinion was only partly medical, called Ulyett a dam' fool for attempting anything so foolish; he was lucky to have any fingers left.

But the catch that is for ever enshrined as the classic catch of all time was taken by poor Fred Grace, W.G.'s youngest brother, in the Oval Test match of 1880. This was Fred's first and last Test, for he died a fortnight later. Bonnor hit a slow ball from Alfred Shaw upwards with almost superhuman force. Up and up it rocketed into space. The batsmen ran one, ran two . . . They were embarking on a third when the ball started coming down. With flawless judgment Fred had run round to a position in front of the second gas-holder. His heart almost stopped beating as he watched the ball swooping downwards, but he held on to it and Bonnor was out. As he strode up the pavilion steps, a comrade offered sympathy.

'Hard luck, Bon.'

'Hard luck nothing,' growled the rueful giant. 'I should have *hit* the perisher!'

These are the classic occasions on which Bonnor was caught. He never married. An amorous and wealthy widow pursued him from England to Australia, but he escaped.

He was not to be caught every time.

CHAPTER 11

Fiery Particles

I

ANY explanation of the art of present-day bowling has to be set down in such technical language that the layman automatically (and prudently) fights shy of the task. We live in the age of specialization, even in nonsense, and maybe this is inevitable. At the beginning of this doleful century it was not so. Without any particular refinements in classification you could still divide bowling into two main kinds: fast and funny, and though time has marched on, this division, whatever the purist may say of it, is still the most convenient. The assault on the batsman's castle must be carried out by violence or by low cunning. There are perhaps combinations and permutations of the two forms, as when the Surrey and England slow bowler, Tony Lock, bowls his faster ball. (Mr. Lock puts as much fury into the bowling of his slowest ball as most fast bowlers put into their fastest.) Nevertheless, one of the most satisfying human acts is that of hurling things at other things, particularly things that will break. An elderly lady of my acquaintance, sweet and gentle in a Victorian way, has confessed to me that her idea of perfect bliss would be an option on a giant pile of bricks, all ready and waiting to be flung at plate-glass windows. The thing is not explicable, except in Freudian terms, which, in my view, do not constitute an explanation. If fast bowlers enjoy bowling very fast, good luck to them. It may be that they regard their task as an uncongenial one which must be gone through in order to obtain their wages, but I doubt this.

A fast bowler is, at any rate ideally, a simple soul. He is seldom an intellectual, as your true slow bowler is bound to be. I do not use the word *intellectual* as an insult, though some who claim the title for themselves tend to make it so. I merely mean a man with a mind, a man like Wilfred Rhodes or Colin Blythe. These men spent their cricketing lives eternally pitting their keen and subtle minds against the enemy's. If you look at a photograph of Hedley Verity, you will see the features of a young man of fine character and keen intellect. I admit there are exceptions, for Hesketh Prichard, though swift and hostile as a bowler, was undoubtedly a man with a first-class mind. But, very broadly speaking, a fast bowler can more aptly be described as a child of Nature. Not for him the subtly varied plan of campaign which lures the batsman to self-destruction. The fast bowler wants to see the bails fly. Just as the Fat Boy wanted to 'make yer flesh creep', so the fast bowler likes to hear the crash of timber. The thing is elemental and instinctive. Do I over-simplify? Of course I over-simplify, but this is the heart of the matter.

Sometimes one wonders how the heroes of old, bowling underhand, could bowl so fast. It is easy to see where the velocity of a Tyson or a Statham comes from, but how did the old 'uns achieve their speed without turning their arms over? Their speed was undoubted. Nyren spoke, almost with bated breath, of the *tremendous* bowling of Thomas Brett, who was 'beyond all comparison the fastest as well as the straightest bowler that was ever known', and delivered the ball 'with the force of a point-blank shot'. Without a shadow of doubt, Brett bowled to hit the stumps and rejoiced mightily at the sound of their downfall.

Brett was a Hambledon man; George Brown was born in Sussex about the time when Brett was bowling his way into history. (I know there was another George Brown, who played for Hampshire about a hundred years later, an all-rounder who could bat, bowl and keep wicket and was probably the most valuable emergency man that England ever fell back on.) But we are now talking of the first quarter of the nineteenth century. Not all fast bowlers have been big men—Larwood was a comparatively small one—but Brown was an eighteen-stone giant of a fellow, six foot three and broad in chest and shoulders. He began his working life as a tailor, but found the occupation unexciting, and took to cricket (and fast bowling) as an outlet to his natural store of nervous energy. For a time he was lessee of the Royal Brighton cricket ground, hence his better-known title, 'Brown of Brighton'. He was the sort of man to whom legends stuck like burrs. His bowling was so swift and terrible that one ball bowled by him at Lord's passed batsman, wicket-keeper, and long-stop, shot right through a coat held out to stop it by an optimistic spectator and killed a dog 'instantaneously, which happened to be at the other side'. 'Little Dench', when standing long-stop to him, filled a sack with straw and stuffed it inside his shirt to protect his chest.

Bowling was Brown's first love and his batting was a form of light entertainment. During the period 1820–30—practically the whole of George IV's belated reign—he turned out for the Players against the Gentlemen; sometimes he went in first and sometimes he went in last, but always, without intermission, he was trying to hit the ball very hard. In fact, he was much the same sort of batsman as Big Jim Smith of Middlesex and must have been an even more terrifying bowler. He lived till his seventy-fourth year and was the father of seventeen children. (I am told by a certain West Indian cricketer's admirers that he will easily beat that, and mine is the charity that believeth all things.) Energy and exuberance. These were George Brown's watchwords.

There is a record of a by-no-means-mythical Mr. Marcon who came down to West Gloucestershire in the early days of the old Grace family to play against the local side two years before W.G. was born. 'Mr. Marcon,' says the inspired record, 'did not trouble about the length of the ball. He aimed at the wicket, and the ball flew straight from his hand to it without touching the ground; and nearly every time it hit the bottom of the stumps, the stump was smashed.'

His habit was not merely to knock the bat out of your hand, but to knock it through your wicket. A fiery particle, indeed.

II

I HAVE written earlier of 'Fearful' Jackson and 'Tear 'em' Tarrant and the terror they spread among their foes. Their bowling was potent and remorseless; they did not so much dismiss their opponents as extirpate them. They wrought fearful carnage among the Eighteens and Twenty-Twos throughout the country, but this, you might say, was only their fun. In county matches, and for the Players against the Gentlemen, they were lethal on level terms. When they bowled on the same side, they presented their foes with a double reason for swift departure.

Jackson, a big man with a beautiful rhythmic action, was a Suffolk man who gravitated to Notts, in contradistinction to so many Nottinghamshire cricketers who gravitated to other counties. As a country boy it was his custom to run barefoot after the hounds and exercise his marksmanship by throwing stones at everything in sight. He was, because of his turbulent temperament, a fiercely fiery particle. At Lord's, where the wickets in his day were as rugged as he was, batsmen required all their courage to stand up to him and twenty years before that great bowler Spofforth appeared on the scene, Jackson was understandably known as 'the Demon'. Everyone knows how when he took a wicket, he blew his nose like the trumpet of a prophecy—a prophecy that further wickets would shortly fall. But if, instead of allowing him to hit your wicket, you lashed out and hit him to the boundary, he felt that he had been insulted. A couple of knocks like that and you had given him his excuse; if he could not bowl you out, he could bump you out. His personal life was almost as uninhibited as his bowling and he sadly ended his days in that purgatory of the Victorian poor, the workhouse infirmary. I have never yet been able to feel that, because a fate is your own fault, it is any the less sad.

Tarrant was neither so resounding a character nor quite such a fine fast bowler as Old Jack, but he was formidable enough. He had much less than Jackson's height, but was equally strong and fast. He was, moreover, equally averse from being punished and would subject any batsman who treated him with disrespect to what was virtually a series of dive-bombing raids. Indeed, his chief difference from Jackson was that, under punishment, he became an angry little man instead of an angry big man. Just as Tom Emmett's motto was supposed to be 'first a wide then a wicket', so Tarrant's motto might have been: 'first a bumper and then a yorker; one over your head and then one under your bat'. In his first Gentlemen v. Players match, at Lord's in 1862, he took seven for 17, and few there were who could stand up to him. But he had other hobbies besides fast bowling and his end was even sadder than Jackson's, for he died at the age of thirty-one.

In mid-century, before W.G. seized the throne and exercised

suzerainty over the Gentlemen *v.* Players series, the Players were almost invariably stronger in bowling, but there were exceptions. In the late 'forties and early 'fifties there was Harvey Fellowes, whom Sir Pelham Warner has described as nearly the fastest, if not the fastest, bowler in history. It is a little hard that, in spite of his excellent record, he is chiefly remembered as (*a*) once having knocked a batsman's large white hat on to his wicket, and (*b*) being the bowler in the famous Gentlemen *v.* Players game in which W. Ridding brought off an incredible feat of stumping. It was a leg-ball of unexampled velocity even for Fellowes, and Ridding whipped off Hillyer's bails as if it had been a slow donkey-drop. I once saw Evans perform a similar near-miracle to this in a Scarborough Gentlemen *v.* Players game. The victim was Doug Insole and the bowler was Alec Bedser. The sight was electrifying, even though Bedser, albeit a finer bowler than Fellowes, was not nearly so fast.

One of the tear-away bowlers of Grace's early days was the left-handed J. C. (Jemmy) Shaw, who over a long period was W.G.'s whipping-boy. Twice in the first over of an important game Shaw got rid of W.G. for naught; in each of his second innings W.G. made well over 200. W.G. had the utmost respect for Jemmy personally, but his respect for his bowling was more limited. *The Dictionary of National Biography* said of Shaw that he once applied to W.G. an epigrammatic description, which, 'divested of some adverbial adornment', ran as follows: 'I puts 'em where I likes,' quoth he, 'but that beggar, he puts 'em where *he* likes!'

Shaw was a reasonably good fieldsman, but, like the rest of us, he sometimes dropped his catches. Once he dropped W.G. His ten fellow-fieldsmen gazed at him in agonized remonstrance, but Jemmy stared back doggedly: 'I like to see the beggar bat.'

Whenever Jemmy tried to induce W.G. to visit the other end, so that he (Jemmy) might have a chance of bowling at some less invulnerable batsman, the Grand Old Man would hit him for four or six or even (if it was the last ball of the over) for five. And when the crowd jeeringly told him that he would never get W.G. out, he would reply stolidly: 'Nobody wants me to, do they?'

Though one of the best bowlers of his day, Shaw was, almost
without competition, an even worse batsman than his unfortunate colleague, Nottinghamshire's next fastest bowler, Fred
Morley. In his career Jemmy took far more wickets than he
was ever likely to make runs. (I make his wickets 1,806 and
his runs 841, but I wouldn't like to argue about it.) For his
county he played, or at least attempted to play, over a hundred
innings and only once rose into the realm of double figures.
His captain in the All England Eleven declared that Jemmy
was never worth four runs against any bowling in his life, but
this is sheer libel against a good man.

In the Gentlemen *v.* Players match at the Oval in 1871, unless scorers and historians made a mistake, he scored 18. This,
for Jemmy, was terrific, in the class of Sir Leonard Hutton's 364
on the same ground sixty-seven years later. The rest of his
batting was not so successful; in his remaining appearances
for the Players he made seven ducks, but, to do him justice,
four of these were not out. When you come to think of it,
'naught, not out,' must have been his favourite score. It may
even be that skilful evasive action between the wickets saved
him the trouble of receiving a single ball.

Yet once in every man's life comes the chance to become a
character in an old-fashioned *Boy's Own Paper* serial and once
in Jemmy's life he played a hero's part. It was when Notts were
playing Gloucestershire at Bristol, and the story is even less
credible than most true stories. At the end of the second day,
Notts, with but one wicket to fall, still needed 43 runs to save
the follow-on. Richard Daft, Nottinghamshire's captain, and
the most elegant batsman of the period, was still in at one
end but who, in the morning, was to fight for the flag at the
other? Who, indeed? Notts's No. 11, who was only No. 11
because there was no No. 12.

It was stated in the Press that Notts's No. 11 did 'not go to
bed at an orthodox hour'. This was untrue, or, at best, a
thumping understatement. Jemmy had not been to bed at all.
He had sat up most of the night in his hotel, drinking beer,
playing cards, drinking beer, quarrelling genially with his
best friends, drinking beer and, eventually, though without
malice, smashing all the glasses in the house and going out into
the night. He was last heard to declare that he would do for

himself and, although this extremity was not deemed to be likely, it appeared only too probable that Notts would be a man short when play began again. As Mr. Daft walked towards the ground the following morning, he reflected sombrely that his side would be forced to follow on straight away and bat a second time a man short, at that. He was informed, however, by one of the Gloucestershire players that a body had been discovered under a tree on the Downs. The body belonged to James C. Shaw and all the evidence underlined the fact that he had passed out as cold as cold could be. There is, however, a special Providence that looks after bodies in such a condition, and in an hour Jemmy was washed, clothed and as nearly in his right mind as was ever likely. Mr. Daft, as we know, was a gentleman of the utmost propriety and he must have strongly disapproved of Jemmy's conduct. Yet he breathed a sigh of relief as they walked out to the wicket. It was statistically improbable that Jemmy would survive an over, but at least it was a major mercy that he was there at all.

Daft, of course, was an astute strategist and did his best to 'farm' the bowling, scoring courageously and artistically, but he could not take every ball at each end. The astonishing thing was that Jemmy was still there. Every ball constituted a miracle of survival. Sometimes he fell on one knee, like a caricature of Jessop, the main difference being that he missed the ball altogether. Sometimes he swung gracefully round in what eighty years later was to be called the Compton sweep and the ball shot past point. If he completely missed the ball, it in its turn missed the stumps by a coat of varnish. If he made a swinging leg hit, it flew over slip's head; if he attempted an off-drive, it skidded harmlessly away to square-leg. The bowlers suffered the torture of a thousand Chinese cuts . . . Before the innings closed Jemmy had written nine epic runs on the scroll of fame and Richard Daft had played a superb innings of 92 not out. Who was then the hero?

As the two returned to the pavilion Jemmy kept glancing stealthily in his captain's direction. He was due for the ticking-off of his life. He braced himself bravely to take what was coming to him. 'Jemmy,' said Mr. Daft sternly, 'I have a word of advice to give you. I've never seen you play so well before.

So I suggest you give up wasting money on hotel beds and sleep in the open air for the rest of the season.'

III

I AM a northerner and it is hard for me not to be more interested in the northern counties than in the others. I have written elsewhere of the famous Kortright[1] of Essex, and whether he was faster than Neville Knox of Surrey or Tyson of our own day no one can say with true authority. There have been fast bowlers in Lancashire from Crossland and Mold, through Kermode and the great Walter Brearley, to Statham and a youngster named Higgs, of whom the present county authorities think highly.   Crossland figures in one of Dick Barlow's favourite stories. Into Barlow's shop came a local yokel.

'Do you,' he asked, 'sell sports equipment?'

'Of course.'

'Then,' said the hero, 'give me a bottle of arnica, a paper of court plaster, and an armsling. This afternoon I'll be batting against Crossland.'

Historically, pre-eminence in Yorkshire bowling has not always been to the swift. Those who toil less and spin more are a different matter. There is a mighty line—almost an imperial dynasty—of slow left-handers who have been, almost without exception, the best of their time: Ted Peate, Bobby Peel, Wilfred Rhodes (the best of *all* time), Roy Kilner, Hedley Verity and Johnny Wardle. (Johnny disclaims all right to be numbered with these giants, but a man can be too modest. His record in South Africa in 1956–57 would make most bowlers proud.) All the world knows these names and knows, too, how they created the legend that the first deliberate act of any male baby born in the West Riding of Yorkshire is to grasp his rattle thoughtfully and project it purposefully from his pram out of the back of his left hand.

But of champion fast bowlers Yorkshire has provided only a few. Hirst was fast—extremely fast in his day—but speed was only one of his rich talents. Bill Bowes was fastish, but he was what his victims called a blinkin' intellectual; that is, he

---

[1] *Cricket My Happiness.*

owed his success less to his speed than to his extremely high intelligence. You must go back a long way to find a fast bowler pure and simple, such as Allan Hill of Lascelles Hall, to whom Tom Emmett used to say: 'All right, Allan, thee *flay* 'em (frighten 'em) out and I'll *ball* 'em out.'

Hill, who was born in Kirkheaton, the birthplace of Hirst and Rhodes, took twelve wickets, all clean bowled in his first county match, and at the Oval.

Go back a little farther and you will discover the man who, said W. G. Grace, was the deadliest fast bowler he ever played against.

George Freeman, who was born at Boroughbridge in early Victorian days, learned his cricket, as a good lad should, from his vicar, Canon Owen, who was an excellent cricketer in his own right. Freeman died all too young, but was in his brief manhood a handsome, trimly-bearded fellow and a superb fast bowler. As a boy bowler he once faced a baronet, a real baronet bold enough to start batting against him in baggy knicker-bockers and no pads. George's first ball hit him on the left leg; his second hit him on the right. At this point the baronet, not unreasonably, demanded leave to retire and don appropriate armour in the pavilion. He then returned, armed *cap à pie*, to the post of peril and was bowled neck and crop by the third ball. That was the sort of innings which, later in his career, George Freeman allowed to much more talented batsmen.

Leaving school, he became a lawyer's clerk, but soon forsook his tall stool for a school-coaching engagement in Scotland, where, playing regularly in club matches, he wrought more havoc than any previous invader since the time of Edward the First. An invitation to play against the powerful All England Eleven brought him temporarily back to Yorkshire and he performed so strikingly that he was asked to join the other side. (He was a man not to be left in an inferior position.) When he started playing for the All England Eleven, he bowled so destructively that to-day some of his figures sound positively frightening. Against one country Twenty-two he bowled seventeen men. This performance included one lurid and annihilating spell in which he took six wickets in eight balls. Against another side he began by blacking the first batsman's eye. With his next nine balls he then took six wickets. He was

not a persistent blacker of eyes. At least I do not think he
enjoyed blacking your eye as Jackson and Tarrant would have
done, it was usually the base of the stumps that he struck,
and he struck them 'mortal hard'.

His career in county cricket was short but dazzling. It
lasted no more than five years but, by the time he came in,
Jackson and Tarrant had departed, and there was no fast
bowler who could seriously challenge a man of his quality. In
the comparatively few first-class matches of these years he took
nearly 250 wickets at a cost of less than nine runs apiece and
he had an average of ten wickets per match.

A vivid picture has come down to us from 1870 of Freeman
bowling, along with Tom Emmett, on the lethal pitch at
Lord's. That was the year when George Summers, of Notts, was
knocked insensible by a heavy blow on the cheekbone from a
rising ball and died three days later. Richard Daft had to receive the next ball sent down and arrived with his head
swathed in towels, as though he were wearing an enormous
turban. Some of his colleagues jeered at his protective clothing,
but not those who were to bat immediately afterwards. On this
same pitch Freeman, with Tom Emmett at the other end,
pounded away at W.G. and his partner. The batting was magnificent, so was the bowling; so were the sunset glories of the
bruises on W.G.'s thighs.

'Tom and I have often said it was a marvel,' George Freeman recalled, 'that the doctor was not maimed or unnerved for
the rest of his days, or killed outright. I often think of his pluck
on that day when I watch a modern batsman scared if a
medium ball hits him on the hand. He should have seen our
expresses flying about W.G.'s ribs, shoulders and head in
1870.'

It was on this ferocious duel that W.G. based his contention
that it was far easier to make a hundred on a friendly wicket
against ordinary bowling than to make fifty on a fiery pitch
against Emmett at his best and Freeman at any time.

'When he hit you on the thigh,' W.G. confided to the young
P. F. Warner, 'it hurt like mad. The ball seemed to sizzle into
your leg, so much spin did he get on her.'

In his last regular season he was picked for the Players
against the Gentlemen at Lord's, where he twice took two

wickets with successive balls and (just to even things up) made only 2 not out. After his retirement he was asked to play once more in the fixture, this time on the Gentlemen's side, but, with a diffidence quite rare in fast bowlers, declined the invitation on the grounds that he was not good enough. Otherwise he would have joined that select band, which included his old acquaintance Richard Daft and ran on, by way of E. J. Diver and the Rev. J. Parsons, to W. R. Hammond and W. J. Edrich, of those who have played on both sides in the series.

When he retired he cheerfully (and prosperously) followed the profession of auctioneer in the cattle market at Thirsk. It sounds sentimental to say that the children of the town loved him, but, at any rate, they were not afraid of him, as so many children were of grown-ups in those days. It was their invariable habit to bring his name into their first daily lesson of mental arithmetic. 'If Mr. Freeman,' they would say, 'sold ten cows at five pounds apiece . . .' This could not have been regularly said of any man who had not won their young hearts.

IV

IT is, at first blush, a far cry from Freeman to Trueman. Freeman lived in a period rich in cricketing characters; Trueman lives, as we all do to-day, in an age which it is customary to write off as virtually characterless. For myself I think that this view, like Mark Twain's demise, has been much exaggerated. Characters may be rare, but those that we have are rare characters. So long as we can see Freddie Trueman on the job, we can retain our confidence. Freddie springs into action, and hope springs with him. Watch him rolling up to the wicket, delivering the ball with his honest cartwheel action, following up with both hands raised in mute appeal (not to the umpire, but to Eternal Justice), flinging back a mane of black hair out of his eyes, and setting out once more on his long return run, as though wondering in a puzzled, exasperated sort of way by what miracle the batsman had survived. Watch all this, I say, and as long as we are privileged to behold it, it is absurd to maintain that cricket has no characters to-day. Observe him as he comes up again in that swaying, trundling, formidably accelerating run. The cartwheel turns. The middle stump flies. (Fancy getting a yorker like that first ball.) He bowls with a fiery resolve never to relax, never to give up, but to get a wicket with just that ball and no other. If you suggested to him that he was mentally quoting Tennyson—'to strive, to seek, to find and not to yield'—he would probably express the intention in his own equally poetic phrase, of clocking you one. He does not, you understand, take a wicket with every ball he sends down, but he makes you feel, as few contemporary bowlers do, that at any moment he might.

England, to put it modestly, is not at this moment badly off for fast bowlers. Apart from Loader, who may become the most accomplished (and the most deadly) of the lot, we have Statham for consistency, Tyson for sheer pace and Trueman for 'devil'. Accuracy can, within reason, be acquired; speed can be stepped up; but 'devil' can no more be evoked at will than spirits from the vasty deep. When Trueman bowled against the Indian touring side of 1952, his impact on them was like the erupting of a volcano. In the following season England kept him up her sleeve until the final Test and, without repeating his Indian massacre, he bowled so aggressively that the back of the Australian batting was broken at a vital juncture, and the Ashes were regained after twenty years. In the 1957 visit of the West Indians he erupted again to take more wickets than any other bowler, his most forceful effort being a destructive spell in the Third Test at Trent Bridge, which forced the West Indies to follow on. It is the possibility of such a devastating burst that makes it worth while always to have such a bowler on your side.

Freeman and Trueman are alike in other accomplishments besides the speed and fury of their bowling. Freeman was a keen and clever fieldsman; so is Trueman, who has practically no equals (outside Surrey) as a snapper-up of unconsidered trifles anywhere 'round the corner'. Freeman, like so many fast bowlers in their moments of relaxation, delighted in free, quick-footed hitting and on many county grounds in the north they will show you the distant trees over which, and the local rivers into which, he drove the best-remembered sixes. An interesting map could be made of these.

Trueman, too, is a happy executant of the gay swing, though he is, in strict fact, far more talented as a batsman than any

No. 9 or No. 10 need be called on to be. It is a statistical fact
that in the 1957 Tests he had a batting average of 89, considerably higher than those of Cowdrey, Richardson and
Sheppard. And if this triumph owed its achievement to the
presence of three not-outs, that was far more to Freddie's credit
than the reverse. Freddie's 1957 batting average was a little
reminiscent of Wardle's in the Tests of England's West Indies
tour of 1953–54, which, if averages are the final proof shows
that Johnny was a better bat than Denis Compton.

If you dreamed that you had seen somebody hit Ramadhin
for three sixes in one over, you would regard the picture, as
you would view the thought of winning £3,000 with your three
Premium Bonds, as a delectable but implausible fantasy. But
with my own eyes at Lord's I saw Trueman do just this and it
was no dream.

Trueman, being human, has had his ups and downs; he has
also had his critics, some of them singularly under-informed.
Of this I should like to say that Freddie has suffered (often
unfairly, I think) from the fierce light that beats upon a vivid
personality. His humour is as broad as his powerful shoulders
and sometimes his vocabulary tends towards Technicolor. It
is impossible for a very fast bowler to avoid giving the batsman
an occasional knock and Trueman has been credited with a
lack of sympathy when this happens. If anyone tells you this,
don't believe it. As a matter of fact, Freddie told me this himself, and I don't believe him.

'Maybe I don't rush up and apologize,' says Freddie, 'and
come to that, when he hits me for six, he doesn't rush up and
apologize neither.'

If anyone thinks this view an inhumane one, I would add
that I have known Freddie pull up his car with a jerk to avoid a
bird in the road. After all, it did not have a bat to defend itself.
The batsman has, and so the fast bowler is licensed, within
reasonable limits, to launch his attacking weapons upon him.

For the fast bowler, as we have said, there abide these three:
accuracy, speed and 'devil'. The greatest of these is 'devil' and
fiery, forthright Freddie Trueman is its truest exponent.

CHAPTER 12

Some Eccentric Matches

I

HALF a century ago I used to spend my Saturday's penny on a quarter of Technicolored sweets called Hundreds-and-Thousands, which were sensational in quantity and, if you were young in heart and stomach, pretty sound in quality, too. I am irresistibly reminded of these far-distant delights when I think of the interesting match which was played between Melbourne University and Essendon even longer ago: in point of fact, in the year 1898. Since that date many records have been woven into the warp and woof of cricket history by the eternal Webber, but this game, as the phrase goes, still presents some notable features.

Some people to-day, for instance, deplore the tedium of five-day Test matches: this game extended over the best (or worst) part of three weeks. The contestants did not do battle all day every day, you understand; the match had its being on three successive Saturdays, with the following Wednesday thrown in, and by that time the season was practically over. Players and umpires were all two weeks and four days older, and for all concerned it may well have seemed a good deal longer.

The eleven representing Melbourne University batted first and made 1,094. I will repeat that. One thousand and ninety-four. The contemporary *Wisden* called this the highest total on record. So it was at the time. It was beaten twenty-nine years later, oddly enough in Melbourne, too, when Victoria totted up 1,107 against the visibly-ageing bowlers of New South Wales. In that innings Ponsford made 352 and Ryder 295. Even more remarkable, I think, was Arthur Mailey's bowling analysis: four for 362. With electronic batsmen like Mr. Ponsford you never knew what might happen. All the same, 1,094 seems to me a pretty fair score. Moreover, on that ground there was none of your modern nonsense about 75-yard boundaries. The cir-

cumference of the playing area, we are told, was 554 yards.
Thus, using a simple mathematical formula and hoping that
the arena was reasonably round, we may reckon that the average
boundary was not less that 88 yards from the pitch. There were
no easy fours to be picked up, though, to be quite fair, this
meant just as much running about for the fieldsmen as the
batsmen. Hard pounding, gentlemen, hard pounding.

The first two University wickets fell for a mere 156; after
that, when L. Miller and E. C. Osborne came together, there
was something of a stand. Miller pushed purposefully along to
205 and Osborne had reached a point well past his century.
They raised the total to 453 and were, you might say, as near
to being set as they were ever likely to be, when Miller, like the
delectable Arthur Wood in similar circumstances, lost his
head in a crisis and was caught at the wicket. One of the shortest
stands of the innings came next: it was only 83. Osborne went
on serenely towards his 190 as though he were laying the foundations of a great commercial enterprise, but his new partner,
O'Hara, had a meagre time. You can imagine the spectacle of
Osborne greedily farming the bowling, hitting up seventy gay
runs while O'Hara struggled to make seven. As I see it, this
unequal contest so exasperated O'Hara, probably a wild Irish
character to start with, that he hit his own wicket down in sheer
frustration. By this suicidal act he achieved the distinction of
being the only batsman on the side to score less than 20.

Two further stands of unchallengeable respectability
brought the score rattling along to 828 for six and then the last
of the five century-makers strode out to the middle. His name
was Bullivant and, having come in at the end of the second day,
he showed a marked disposition to stay at the crease all the
third. He soon lost his partner Feilchenfeld, who had completed a brisk, if rather flighty, 176, but the hours rolled by and
life went on inexorably until the books showed 968 for eight.
At this point the tempo slowed down. I was going to say 'unaccountably' slowed down, but the batsmen had their reasons.
With the total standing at 998, it kept on standing. Our friends
were in the nervous nine-hundred-and-nineties and were
taking no chances. There was no relaxing that grim concentration, no careless throwing of caution to the winds. Bullivants
never forget. Maiden over after maiden over was sent down.

The batsmen were fixtures. The bowlers were somnambulists. Even the wicket-keeper wavered; surprisingly, of course, because vigilance is the badge of all his tribe. Wearily he dozed off; a ball slipped past him for four byes and the unbearable tension eased. There followed a cheerful stand for the tenth wicket and the end came when the last man was caught at 1,094 by a colleague from his own side, fielding as substitute. (There was a certain appropriateness in this. It almost seemed as though he had to be dismissed by a friend: his enemies had lost their confidence.) But at least the innings had finished. Now the labourers' task was o'er and the morning and the evening were the third day.

The bowling analysis should have been set to music: it is an epic in itself. Never in the field of human conflict can so many have been put on for the loss of so few. Eleven men wielded bats and 263.3 overs were sent down, one of them by the wicket-keeper. There is something disturbing here. You would think that, once the stumper had been prevailed on to take off his pads, he might at least have been allowed a fairer chance of self-expression. Why did his captain let him bowl no more than one over? Surely he would have improved in time. In the whole of the innings there were only five wides and there is no proof that he bowled all five of them in his one lone over. No, I suspect jealousy was at work. There is a parallel instance in W. G. Grace's observation during the 1896 Manchester Test to Lilley after that illustrious wicket-keeper had doffed his gloves to take a turn with the ball. He did not gate-crash history as sensationally as that earlier England wicket-keeper, Alfred Lyttelton, who, in the 1884 Test at the Oval, took four for 19 with lobs almost, you might say, before the batsmen noticed he had got his pads off. But Lilley did his best. His first over yielded fourteen runs and a wide, but soon after that he got a wicket and Lilley could never think why the Old Man took him off. 'Put those gloves on, Dick,' said W.G., 'you must have been bowling with the wrong arm.' I cannot but suspect jealousy. The Essendon wicket-keeper resumes his pads with dignity and passes from our ken a much-wronged man.

The heroes of the attack—call it a siege—were the brothers H. and C. Christian. Their combined bowling figures (H. and C.) were: 90 overs, 25 maidens, 2 wickets, 280 runs. Did those great twin brethren, the Bedsers, ever display such Christian endurance? I have set down H. and C. as brothers, though this is not necessarily so. They may have been father and son; indeed, as the thousand mark approached and time faded into eternity, they may have felt like grandfather and grandson. H. Christian's individual tally was the starker of the two: 52 overs, 23 maidens, 1 wicket, 243 runs. He may have imagined that these heroic figures would remain a record for all time. It is sad to think that, had he lived till 1951—and he need only have been about seventy—he would have seen this record shattered by that remarkable bowler of our own day, J. J. Warr, of Middlesex and England, who in Tests in the 1950–51 tour of Australia won for himself the following awe-inspiring analysis: 73 overs (584 balls), 6 maidens, 1 wicket, 281 runs. I have heard Mr. Warr express indignation towards a sceptical critic who questioned the number of runs. 'No,' he murmured austerely, 'I remember the figure exactly. Hymns Ancient and Modern No. 281, *Art thou weary, art thou languid, art thou sore distressed?*'

One record of the 1898 match, however, remains unassailable to this day. There has never been another instance of eleven bowlers joining in the attack in a single innings, with five of them each having over a hundred runs hit off him. These were they who passed through great tribulation. The bowling heroes were not so heroic with the bat. Everybody cannot do everything. There can be few single innings matches that have been lost by over a thousand runs. This was one of them. Our heroes' total against their opponents 1,094 reached only 76. Two men scored twenty runs. These were W. Griffiths, who had already proved his mettle by taking two wickets for 137, and C. Dalton, who had bowled only ten overs and must have been fresher. The most doleful part of the story is that the match died with the fall of the seventh wicket and the tail of the scoresheet reads:

W. Smith (absent) ...	...	...	...	0
C. Sampford (absent)	...	...	...	0
J. Gaunt (absent) ...	...	...	...	0

What happened to these missing persons? One is tempted for each of them to echo the gibes that the prophet Elijah threw at the prophet of Baal: Perchance he is pursuing, or he is in a journey, or peradventure he sleepeth, and must be awaked? Poor Smith, poor Sampford, poor Gaunt . . . Had they gone on strike? Had they fallen into a state of coma? Had they just come to dislike cricket? The man who draws out my deepest sympathy is C. Christian, who at the moment of high crisis, when his comrades deserted the stricken field, was 13 not out. You can just imagine him musing in the pavilion afterwards, in his mild, wistful Australian way. 'There was I, chum, well set, and only 1,019 to get to win. If I'd only had somebody to stay with me we'd have got 'em, too right, we would.' He probably ended by thinking 13 an unlucky number.

II

WHENEVER we think of the harsh rigours of the English climate, which is at its cruellest in May, we might spare a thought for those who endured the period of which *Wisden* wrote, not without emotion: 'All England will remember with a shiver and a shudder, the long, sad and severe winter of 1878–79, commencing as it did, in October, '78, and continuing with more or less severity up to the middle of May, '79, and even then the cold, nipping, bronchitis-creating winds seemed loth to leave the land they had so sorely stricken with distress, disease and death. But there is no black cloud without its silver lining, and one bright spot in this dark winter was that its severity and length enabled more cricket matches on the ice to be played than were ever before played in the course of one winter . . .'

All over the country matches were played on ice: at Hull, Grimsby and Eridge Castle, Kent; on a dam near Chesterfield and on a marsh near Gainsborough; by members of the Sheffield Skating Club on the Duke of Devonshire's Swiss Cottage pond and on the frozen lake in the Earl of Scarbrough's Park. There were two other matches. One was played by moonlight in Windsor Park and it sent the local chronicler in romantic mood. He must have been the first poet to hymn in prose 'the long glories of the winter moon'.

'The moon was full on the 8th Jan.,' he wrote, 'shining with unclouded and truly splendid brightness throughout that evening and night. At the same time a sharp, keen, thoroughly old-fashioned frost was setting the ice in capital form for skating and other icy pastimes. The next day being bright, frosty, and fine, the skating cricketers of the royal borough announced their intention . . .'

There was a 'gate' of several hundred spectators and they derived 'no end of amusement' from the plight of the players. Scoring was not prolific, one side making fifteen and the other, with ten men, beating them by two runs. The gusts of happy laughter which sent the spectators rolling in the snowdrifts on the boundary were caused by the difficulties encountered by the players on three counts: batting, bowling and fielding.

One match of the winter season was more interesting than the others, if only because it was played between Cambridge Town and Cambridge University. At the game in Windsor Home Park the crowd laughed because most of the players simply could not skate and the figures they cut on the ice were just nobody's business. In Cambridgeshire, flattest of the Fen-land counties, skating is no nine winters' wonder, as it is in shires less blest, but a genuinely popular pastime, where ex-pertize is the normal thing. In most of the other games it was ruled that batting required less dexterity than bowling and fielding and that therefore a man should make 25 runs quickly and then retire. This principle produced some oddly egali-tarian score-cards in which practically everybody on both sides was 25 not out.

In the Cambridge match there was none of this nonsense. The Town team were accomplished skaters to a man; when they won the toss they began to score freely and at the end of the evening's play (two hours) they had scored just under 200, with two wickets still to fall. But what wickets! One belonged to Dan Hayward the Second, a senior member of Cambridge's most illustrious cricketing family, who was later to be Ranji's winter coach. (Ranji wore fur gloves while batting and Dan pegged down his right leg to teach him—bless my soul—defen-sive strokes.) The other champion was Carpenter, frequent partner of Dan's brother, Tom, and a loyal member of both Wandering Elevens. When Carpenter had finished banging the bowling about, his own score was 89 and the Town's total was 326.

It seems that when the University's innings began 'the ice was very bad', but after the fall of one cheap wicket Nos. 2 and 3 managed to survive. On the third evening the ice must have 'rolled out' well, or frozen smoothly over, and so the batsmen vigorously set about the bowling until, with the fall of three more wickets, the score was taken to 274 for four, and left there. At the finish the brothers Pigg (H. and C.) were still batting briskly for 69 and 39 not out and though the Townsmen made strenuous efforts to huff and puff and blow their house down, the little Piggs remained safe.

The most striking thing about this match is not the skilful skating of all concerned, but the place where they skated, which comprised twenty acres of land, flooded by their owner, at Grantchester. When we consider the big hitting indulged in by Hayward and Carpenter on one side and the Piggs on the other, we wonder in our innocent way about the size of their hits and whether it was Bob Carpenter who 'clocked' the church clock with a tremendous six. It would have been a fascinating triumph of critical literary research to discover who, nine years before the poet was born (and obviously in the middle of the night), stopped the church clock at ten to three.

III

You will remember Sir Aubrey Smith, the tall, handsome Englishman who went into films and, late in life, became the uncrowned king of Hollywood. Even Hollywood is not wrong about everything and, when it came to regard Sir Aubrey as its ideal of a fine old English gentleman, it showed more than usual intelligence. Long before that time, though few can recall it now, he had been C. A. Smith, of Cambridge University, Sussex and England, and captain of M.C.C.'s first touring side in South Africa. He was a slow bowler—slow to the point of slow motion—who used to start his run about mid-off and then, as though by an afterthought, bowled round the wicket. That is why they called him 'Round-the-Corner' Smith and his house in Hollywood was christened *Round the Corner*. In the film colony he ran his own cricket team, and he ran it as strictly as Lord Hawke or Lord Harris would have done. He was a stickler, as you may imagine, for etiquette and insisted on the correct interpretation of cricket's laws, both social and sport-ing, on all occasions. As he grew older, he grew stricter; as he grew older, too, his eyesight grew sketchier and one day in the field he committed the enormity, so hard to forgive in others, of dropping a slip catch. Instantly he stopped the game and sig-nalled for his butler, who walked ceremoniously across the ground and bowed low.

'Bring me my spectacles,' ordered Sir Aubrey.

Slowly the butler returned to the outer world and once more appeared, bearing a pair of spectacles (in case) on a silver salver. Sir Aubrey put on his spectacles and signalled to the umpires permission to resume action. The bowler bowled, the batsman snicked, the ball shot into Sir Aubrey's hands and shot out again. There was an almost interminable pause. Finally a loud complaint arose to heaven: 'Egad,'[1] exclaimed Sir Aubrey, 'the dam' fool brought my reading glasses.'

One day Sir Aubrey's team were scheduled (spell it with a k) to meet a side from a visiting British cruiser and an acquaint-ance of mine had had his name put down to play for the home side. Unhappily, just before the game was due to start he slipped and twisted his ankle. This was no riotous studio party; it happened on a slippery polished floor at a peaceful story con-ference, but the consequences and complications were just the same. He was so utterly scared of Sir Aubrey, who could be a merciless martinet, that he simply dared not confess to him what had happened. His only hope, he felt, was at all costs to produce a substitute. He therefore hobbled round Hollywood on the arm of a girl friend in a desperate search for some guy who could play this English game of cricket. Try as they might, the only man they could get hold of was the actor, William Boyd, the creator of Hopalong Cassidy, ten-gallon hat, top-boots, cowboy's pony and all. Or so my friend told me.

Hopalong disclaimed the faintest notion of how to play cricket, but they assured him that it was a simple game, closely resembling baseball, only not so complicated, and at last they persuaded him to put on flannels, though, now I come to think of it, it may well have been a mistake not to suggest that he should take his spurs off first. Fortunately, when they reached

[1] I have always held that no human creature in this century ever used the word *Egad*. I was wrong. Sir Aubrey did.

the cricket ground, Sir Aubrey had already won the toss and decided to bat, so nobody had especially observed either the absence of the injured man or the identity of the substitute. My friend being a bowler, Hopalong was kept back till No. 9 in the batting order and when he went rolling out to the wicket, all six feet three of him, he presented an imposing spectacle.

There he stood at the crease, swinging his bat in one hand as though it were a policeman's truncheon. The umpire politely asked if he wanted centre.

'Start pitchin',' commanded Hopalong.

The first ball he missed; the second he missed; the third was a nice slow full toss on the leg side and from it he hit a towering skier away in the broad direction of long-on, possibly into Beverly Hills, and even, for all I know, into the Pacific Ocean.

Suddenly, to the horror of all the Englishmen present, Hopalong went mad. Without a word he dashed across to point, from point to cover, from cover to mid-off, from mid-off round the astonished umpire to mid-on, from mid-on to square-leg and then, without reflecting on his latter end, slid like a toboggan into his own wicket.

There was as breathless a hush as ever fell on Newbolt's Close. Every trueborn Englishman waited in panic-stricken silence to hear what the outraged Sir Aubrey would say. Finally he exclaimed: 'Well, I declare!'

And, on reflection, that was the most useful thing he could have said.

IV

You can argue as long as you like about which was the greatest, the most exciting, or the strangest Test match. The result of your argument, which will be a draw, will depend on your age and partisan sympathies. Few cricket-lovers over sixty will allow any game ever played to have been greater or more exciting than Jessop's match, the Oval Test against the 1902 Australians, in which Jessop scored a hurricane century and England won, against all probability, by one wicket, Hirst and Rhodes ('We'll get 'em in singles') being undefeated at the end.

Probably, for those who are old enough, the most heart-stopping game was the Manchester Test of the same season, which England lost by three runs. I have a friend who places the blame for this disaster on the shoulders of Lord Hawke, who, as Yorkshire had already contributed three men to the selected twelve, would not allow Schofield Haigh to be added to it. This caused Fred Tate, of Sussex, to be brought in and on the first morning Hirst was relegated to the post of twelfth man. This gave poor Tate his first and last Test match, in which he failed as a bowler, dropped a catch at a vital moment and, coming in to bat under nerve-racking conditions when eight runs were needed to win, hit a four and was bowled. I should hate to blame Tate, a tragic figure who had more to put up with than Hamlet in more distressing circumstances. I certainly would not blame him. I would rather blame Lord Hawke but, if we are to seek scapegoats so far away, how far are we to go? Why not blame Oliver Cromwell?

It may well be that, for the strangest Test match, we need not go back nearly so far. It may be that a generation which grows bored with avuncular chatter about Jessop's match will claim that the strangest Test was Laker's match at Manchester in 1956. In that game Laker took nine for 37 and ten for 53. (9 + 10 = 19.) Fantastic, fantastic, fantastic! If, however, you want for your collection a match which ran the whole gamut of human emotions, I cannot think of any game that could equal the Test against the West Indies at Edgbaston in 1957. This game had everything the connoisseur could desire: a fine ground, enlarged and improved, gorgeous weather, glorious batting, some devastating bowling, an heroic struggle by the side which, by all reasonable probabilities, was doomed to inevitable defeat, a stubborn, proud and splendid recovery, an unaccountable collapse by the side that had been bound to win, and a pulsating finish in which the West Indies' Nos. 8 and 9 just managed to defend their wickets until the end of the day. The crowd went home tingling with excitement and muttering might-have-beens to themselves: 'If Tony Lock could have had one more over, we'd have won.' For myself, I came away with that odd feeling that I have occasionally experienced before, when witnessing in real life some fantastically dramatic game which, as a writer of fiction, is no use to me whatever. Editors are predictably pessimistic chaps.

'Come, come,' they will say. 'Be plausible. Spare us this tissue of unlikelihoods. Save them for your schoolboy serials . . .'

Ah, well, here undoubtedly was the match of the season, played against touring opponents who, on their previous visit, had wasted the land with fire and slaughter. Worrell, Weekes and Walcott, the dark and terrible hammers of the English. the batsmen whom nobody could get out; Ramadhin and Valentine, the unplayable bowlers who had entered not merely into legend, but into Caribbean folk-song. The sun shone as it seldom shines in Birmingham and the turf looked as if it had been prepared by Messrs. Burroughs & Watts. It was a good toss to win and England's captain won it. He must have sighed with relief and speculated, on such a wicket, whether to declare the next day around lunch-time at 400 or 500. (Or must he? He is a very sober-minded young gentleman.) England's two left-handed batsmen started off briskly and when lunch was taken at 93 for two, spectators were reasonably contented, even if they had been subjected to few excitements.

I do not know what Ramadhin had for lunch. Perhaps it was his favourite curry. It is unlikely that he ate a dynamite salad, but his effect upon the batsmen was explosive. Within less than an hour on that beautiful wicket he had, by diabolically clever variations of pace and flight, taken five wickets for nine runs, and if Trueman had not come in to fight a characteristically swashbuckling, analysis-battering rearguard action, Ramadhin's figures would have been even more startling. Even after Trueman's belated hammering, he finished with seven wickets for 49, an astonishing feat on a batsman's pitch. The flower of England's batting had bitten the dust, or would have done if that perfect wicket had been at all dusty. In a five-day match this feeble batting was as near suicide as was possible. When West Indies retired for the day at 83 for Pairaudeau's wicket—he was yorked by Trueman—they were a mere hundred runs behind and were plainly ready to build up a massive total in the morning. Mr. Barrington Dalby would have awarded them full first-round points.

The second day provided something for everybody's requirements. A wicket fell to Statham's first ball and then the burly Walcott became a victim of cramp and was granted a runner. Weekes joined him and the batting was of the kind to make the bowlers despair: an impenetrable defence to every good ball and a rocket-driven four off any ball the least bit over- or under-pitched.

The crowd roared when Trueman bowled Weekes and oohed like soccer fans when the new-comer, Sobers, in two successive bursts of initial insobriety, appeared bent on running himself out. Perhaps these escapes steadied him: almost at once he began to play beautifully, less solidly, perhaps, than Walcott but, as it turned out, just as effectively. They were only three runs behind England's score when Walcott was joyously snapped at the wicket and only eleven in front when Bailey leaped like an Olympic diving champion to catch Sobers. England's reviving supporters passionately felt that at this point their men should have seized the enemy by the throat and shaken the life out of him, but Collie Smith and Worrell (with runner) refused to be shaken. At close of play the two had added 119, not by painful defence but by relentless, though far from reckless, hitting. Full points once more were due to West Indies. And so to Round Three.

I do not remember seeing a cricket ground more tightly packed than was the Edgbaston 'gate' the following (Saturday) morning. Immediately below where I sat was a gay, witty, richly vocal Caribbean contingent, supported by a melodious steel band. It almost seemed as if they had brought the blazing sunshine with them. The huge English crowd, like any other collection of English citizens in this age, seemed full of goodwill, fair-mindedness and anxiety in about equal proportions.

The batting was so remorseless that you had to watch every ball closely to observe how keen and courageous was the attack, whether delivered by Statham, Trueman, Bailey, Laker or Lock. Each of them bowled at the top of his own high talents, quick or slow, fierce or crafty. With the last ball before lunch Statham performed the miracle of removing Worrell's off bail without appearing to touch the stumps. West Indies were two hundred in front and, so far as their chances went, on velvet, richly piled.

Remorseless is the word. With some ready help from his captain, Smith went on to make a century in his first Test in England. It was a glorious day in the life of young Collie Smith, who had set about the bowling as if he meant to whack it into insensibility. It was a beautiful day, too, in the lives of his fellow-

Caribbeans there assembled. The only lives in which the day, or that moment of it, was not so happy were those of the City of Birmingham police, whose delicate duty it was to prevent poor Collie from being trampled to death by his admirers. These in their thousands were seized by an overmastering desire to dash across the ground and shake his hand, removing it, if necessary, from the wrist, elbow or even shoulder, in the process. For an instant a beautifully ugly situation seemed about to develop, but authority held—Birmingham, your police are wonderful!—Collie waved his bat and then went on to bat at a faster pace than ever. As West Indies began to hurry, so their end came appreciably nearer. Goddard was astonishingly caught by Lock, high above his head, in the unwonted position of deep mid-on. (If Lock were fielding behind the heavy roller, he would still field better than any man in England.) Smith was out at last, l.b.w. to Laker, for 161; Atkinson was beautifully caught in the deep by Statham, who also threw out the last man from so great a distance that the ball seemed like a guided missile. West Indies were out, but they were 288 in front. Has any Test side started its second innings nearly 300 runs behind and survived? Hardly. It did not help when England lost two wickets (rather unnecessarily, I thought) by six o'clock and Ramadhin was again the villain. It seemed at that instant that England would again be rolled in the dust.

I wonder what Peter May was thinking when he came down the pavilion steps. I have been this young man's somewhat slavish admirer ever since I first saw him as a schoolboy. It is impossible not to admire his quiet courtesy off the field and his cool mastery on it. It is deceptively possible for a young man to be well-mannered and friendly and yet to have articulated steel as part of his composition. That mastery was urgently needed now. He might have put up the shutters or, as Patsy Hendren would have phrased it, hidden behind his bat, hoping for mere survival, which might allow him to fight again another day. So far from defending doggedly, he flung out a gage of defiance and hit two rasping fours between cover and mid-off that almost scorched the grass as they flew to the rails. I have never seen a batsman show more individual confidence where it seemed that so little could be hoped for.

Close was out fairly early on the Monday morning, and then

began the stand that went on until teatime on the Tuesday, the best part of two days. It did not end till Cowdrey at last grew tired of hitting fours and holed out a little short attempting a six. Systematically, May and Cowdrey set about subjugating the bowling, wearing it down from morn till noon, from noon till dewy eve; from lunch till tea, from tea till close of play. If the record of this recovery sounds monotonous, I have set it down wrongly. It was a battle and in the beginning the two Englishmen were slowly, relentlessly fighting their way out of an impossible position, but they never looked as though they were indulging a forlorn hope. Even when Ramadhin bowled five successive maidens, the batsmen played them firmly. Clean defensive strokes were made in such a way as to suggest that they would deal with the matter firmly later on. Their motto appeared to be: take no risks, but hit hard anything that can be hit.

As time passed the bowlers grew tired, but the batsmen did not. Cowdrey began to score at a quickened pace and May kept on at roughly twice the speed. Neither batsman owed anything to fortune. It was a triumph of concentration, personal courage and stamina, piled on top of splendid skill. After an astonishing day's cricket England were 378 for three and 90 in front.

The two were still together at lunch on the fifth and final day and it was well into the afternoon when Cowdrey was caught on the rails by one of the small army of substitutes. May and Cowdrey had scored 411 for the fourth wicket (and broken all kinds of records) and they had brought England's chances back, not so much from the brink of the grave as from about ten feet underground. Godfrey Evans came out to display his own brand of boyish fun and at 583 for four May declared. His personal score was 285 not out and to spray his achievement with the ordinary adjectives of commerce is to damn it with faint praise. Old men remember Jessop's match of 1902; some even remember Ranji's match of 1896. Some remember Hobbs and Sutcliffe in 1926 and many remember Hutton in 1938. Great men, great deeds. But here is another great man, or I'm a Dutchman! With great respect to them all, and to Bradman, Compton, Hammond and the other giants, May's innings was, considering the desperate situation in which it was born,

among the best half-dozen innings ever played by anyone, anywhere. And Cowdrey was a partner of true valour and worth.
Ramadhin had bowled ninety-eight overs. If ever a man was
prematurely aged it was he.

Often in history such a recovery is followed by an anti-
climax, with so little time in which to achieve a result. This is
the sort of stage at which the spectators, worn out by drama and
bored by the prospect of inevitable bathos, totter home yawn-
ing while the wicket-keeper is put on to bowl lobs to entertain
the faithful but dozing remnant. None of these things happened. On the contrary, the astonishing Peter May, whose grateful country might at this moment have thought of awarding
him a peerage and allowing him to go away for a rest cure,
was seen, not content with an honourable draw, to be going
all out for a win. It was a Churchillian gesture: 'Our aim—
victory.'

Close took a dazzling catch on the rails to a stroke that might
have gone for six; Trueman, in the Trueman manner, knocked
a stump out of the ground; and Lock deceived Sobers with a
going-away ball, which went away to some purpose into
Cowdrey's hands at slip.

The West Indies had much food for sombre thought at tea
and more indigestive matter immediately afterwards. May
himself caught Worrell for a duck and four wickets were down
for twenty-seven. England were striding towards victory. It was
a strange and unearthly sight to see such storming warriors as
Walcott and Weekes desperately defending their stumps, as
every ball brought our hearts into our mouths. Where the
batsmen's hearts were it is difficult to say, but Walcott was
caught by Lock at 43. England were pressing inexorably towards a final triumph and the fieldsmen aggressively moved in
closer, seeking suicide catches even in the cannon's mouth.
It is always a heartening sight to see Lock fielding; it was awe-
inspiring to see the other English fieldsmen, inspired by Lock,
fielding *like* Lock. It was Trueman who took the next catch
when Weekes, whose defensive play had been a model to his
colleagues, edged a particularly unpleasant ball from Lock to
slip. Sixty-one for six. This was the top of the curve, the zenith
of England's upsurge towards triumph. Goddard came in and
played with the defiance of a man who would die rather than

lose his wicket. (If his pads tended to appear his first line of
defence and his bat the second, the umpire could not agree
with Lock that there was anything immoral about this.) History records two or three notable innings of naught not out.
Among those immensely valuable contributions, Goddard's
stands high. Five minutes from time Collie Smith was cruelly
deceived by Laker, but it was now too late for England to
snatch the win they had come to deserve. In the remaining
moments Atkinson hit a four through a ring of fieldsmen and
the match ended in a draw. But, by heaven, it did not peter out.
It began in glory; it rose to almost unscalable heights and it
went out, blazing.

The captains and the kings depart; the critics never. There
were those who asked (churlishly, I think): should not May
have declared earlier? Did he really go out for a win from the
start of the West Indies innings, or only after the first couple
of wickets had fallen quickly? I sympathize with any captain's
hesitation in declaring when he had the three W's, plus Sobers
and Collie Smith against him, eager to dash in and knock off
the runs. It may be that England's captain saw the object of
the match as the complete subjugation of Ramadhin, because,
after their wretched first innings, England must achieve that
objective or perish. England did not perish and this paved the
way for overwhelming victory in the series. If in those closing
moments England could have secured ten wickets instead of
seven, it would have been a glorious victory, but it was a
glorious finish, anyway.

During the course of this match a friend of mine was in an
'amenity' bed in hospital and on a small portable radio set he
listened to the game from start to finish. An old gentleman,
awaiting an operation in another ward, slipped out of bed and
listened in the corridor to my friend's radio. When invited in,
he spent several hours of the first three days of the match in my
friend's room. On the Monday morning he underwent his
operation, and did not come round till the evening. As he
emerged from unconsciousness he murmured: 'Is May still in?'

The doctor, who had more accomplishments than mere
surgery, told him.

Over the old gentleman's face spread a serene expression
similar to that which accompanied the last words of General

Wolfe on the Heights of Abraham: 'Thank God, I can die happy.'

'What a boy!' (or possibly 'Attaboy!') he murmured blissfully and passed out.

I am happy to report that he had recovered sufficiently to be at the Oval three weeks later. And his return to normal must have been complete—he was heard grumbling at the selectors.

Some of our newspaper correspondents, those creators of the flashing phrase, described May's innings as a 'captain's knock'. Goddard's, yes, and all honour to him. But May's? No. If May's 285 not out, in a match which had been virtually lost when he went in, was a captain's knock, then Columbus was a bit of a navigator.

CHAPTER 13

My Step-Uncle Walter

It was a childish ignorance,
But now 'tis little joy
To know I'm farther off from heaven
Than when I was a boy.

THOMAS HOOD

IT was Kipling's soldier who went out into the world so wide 'for to admire and for to see' and to learn about women from various sources. Similarly, though less adventurously, I have learnt about cricket from many people: from reading Old Ebor and Neville Cardus; from watching cricket's great historic pageant during my fortunate lifetime, a pageant that for me began with Ranji and Jessop and now sweeps along from Hutton and Compton to May and Cowdrey; from listening to the gruff wisdom of such good men as Hirst and Rhodes (and none better bowled a ball); and from chatting with such lively characters as my friend Johnny Wardle. I have even played a bit myself. But I should never have learnt about cricket at all if my education had not received its grounding from my Step-Uncle Walter. Stephen Leacock was not the only man to have a remarkable uncle. I had one, too.

My own forebears were Scots and I have no drop of blood in my veins that is not as Scottish as Scotch. My great-grandfather came south from Argyllshire and my grandfather was for over fifty years 'Wee Free' minister in Galashiels, the Border town where, as they will tell you to this day, they *lear-rned* Wilfred Rhodes to play cricket. My mother died when I was four years old and my father, whose work had brought him to Yorkshire, afterwards married a Yorkshirewoman who discharged with extreme conscientiousness her duties towards what the period sentimentally called her motherless child. Thus I became heir to two traditions. Of the Scottish tradition of love of country and of learning I will not speak here, except to say that I deem it the greatest in history. On a less-exalted level, the Yorkshire tradition of my boyhood was also truly admirable. Sociologists, with their unerring flair for the fatuous, would no doubt have described it as 'collective adherence to the myth of the group behaviour pattern'. It was a tradition of penury, duty, nonconformity in religion and thrift. True, at its worst, the duty could be irksome, the nonconformity could be a mere conformity to something else less kindly, and the thrift could degenerate into downright meanness; but, at its best, the tradition was a high one. In any event, it called for some sort of loyalty and some sort of grit. In this bleak corner of a northern field that was for ever Yorkshire, my Uncle Walter flourished.

In the world of to-day it is fantastic to think that only two wars ago there were people in the world like my Step-Uncle Walter and my Aunt-Martha-by-courtesy. Together they kept a small hotel in the prim, trim spa town in which we lived. They employed an assistant cook and two elderly maids, but my uncle and aunt appeared to do a good proportion of the work themselves. The 'grand' rooms were spotless, though heavily over-furnished in a plushy Victorian manner, and the business prospered, the economy of the country being what it was before the economists got at it. Asked to define the division of labour in the establishment, Uncle Walter would say: 'Martha's the brains and I'm the Boots.'

There were some who regarded Uncle Walter as a meek, ineffectual, henpecked little man, but for me he was kindly authority and unchallenged wisdom. In my eyes he bristled with splendid accomplishments. His skill as a polisher of visitors' boots (and shoes, but mostly boots) was literally dazzling. You could see your own face, though slightly distorted, in the toe-caps of the boots on which he had so brilliantly operated. He could clean silver and polish knives (by rubbing them on a board powdered with bath-brick) and he could sharpen the official carving knife on the second area step till it was brightly lethal as Saladin's scimitar. He could also whistle the tunes of many of Ira D. Sankey's *Sacred Songs and Solos* in a spirited manner that would have delighted the heart of C. T. Studd. His domestic duties were performed in what was called the 'cellar-kitchen', a large airy room at the foot of the area steps, and during my school holidays I would slip away from my own perfectly comfortable home after breakfast to watch Uncle Walter at his polishing. Sometimes before lunch (which I called dinner) I would watch him carve the joints which were to be carried in processional state up to the ground and first floors and, as I gazed, I never ceased to marvel at his artistry. A roast chicken would fall apart under his knife as though touched with a magic wand.

Normally (and formally) he wore discreetly striped trousers, a white shirt with severely turned down collar and bow-tie, and a morning coat that looked rather long because his legs were rather short. While on polishing duty below stairs he protected the striped trousers with a baize apron and exchanged the morning coat for a long-sleeved waistcoat, rather like Sam Weller's in the old prints. Sometimes he would permit me to practise with his brush on a boot of lesser social importance. This was a generous privilege, but, far more generously, he opened for me windows in heaven. Never were casements more serenely magic. It was Uncle Walter who brought cricket into my young life.

Uncle Walter was a naturally conscientious worker, and had little leisure for frivolous pursuits. His wants, so to speak, were small. All he claimed for himself was his summer Saturday afternoons. These he spent playing for the cricket team which constituted a slightly surprising by-product of the chapel he and Aunt Martha attended on Sundays. As an additional perquisite, he felt entitled to annex the odd day, or possibly two, in the season to be dedicated to watching Yorkshire's match played on our town ground or even as far away as Leeds or Bradford. Uncle Walter might be a meek little man, but he upheld his privileges like a lion. For my part, it was at first privilege enough to accompany him to his chapel team matches. On cricketing Saturdays he presented a different, but still dapper, appearance, clad in a high-necked white sweater of the type worn by goal-keepers in team-photographs of the period, and a pair of spotless flannel trousers. (Aunt Martha always grumbled automatically as she ironed these every Friday evening but, when she had finished, the creases in them matched the edge of the family carving knife.) We now live in an age when blazers are your only wear, when practically every male person between seven and seventy, always excepting members of the Vincent Club, wears on almost every occasion a blazer with a badge of kaleidoscopic splendour. Not so, Uncle Walter. Instead of a blazer, he wore before going into action an ancient and very tight Norfolk jacket, of the type then worn by George Bernard Shaw. A small cricket cap was perched on the top of his largish, baldish head and he carried his cricket boots to the scene of conflict in a wicker receptacle which, I afterwards learnt, was a cat-basket left by a careless visitor.

Uncle Walter's team, for reasons unconnected with art, were known as the Primitives and, as a slow bowler, Uncle Walter was the Primitives' pride. I wish I had a film-strip of Uncle Walter in action. His movement was emphatically not a run, neither was it a walk; perhaps it could best be described as a sidle. He came up to the wicket with a slow, quiet step, like a kindly uncle tip-toeing silently into a nursery so as not to wake the baby. His large brown eyes beamed benignly on the batsman through his steel-rimmed spectacles and if there was anything stealthy in his action, it was that of a man who did good by stealth and blushed to find it fame. He bowled left-handed, which was almost a matter of self-respect in the Yorkshire of that period. How could you be a slow bowler if you were *not* left-handed? When he bowled, his arm went so far behind his back that it almost disappeared altogether. Uncle Walter's left arm disappeared farther than Woolley's, farther than Wardle's, nearly as far as Mad-Charlie-Brown-of-Nottingham's. Finally, the ball lobbed forward in such an innocent way that no batsman could believe so kindly a character capable of ever *meaning* to get anybody out. Sometimes the batsman breathed a sigh of relief at the thought of escaping to Uncle Walter's end and getting away from the end which was served by an extremely *primitive*-looking Primitive named Bert who, with his long black hair falling over his eyes, delivered a wild, erratic, primitive ball, which was a terror to long-stops. To exchange the blind fury of Bert's end for Uncle Walter's quiet backwater must have seemed to nervous batsmen like entering harbour after battling through stormy seas. Uncle Walter raised their hopes, revived their confidence, lulled their suspicions, and got them out. Sometimes they were stumped, sometimes they were caught in the outfield, and sometimes they were bowled round their legs. Occasionally he got his man leg-before-wicket, but this he appeared to regret. He appealed apologetically, as of mournful necessity, as though he were a kindly probation officer shaking his head over an incorrigible delinquent: 'This lad had every chance, gentlemen, and it distresses me to call for the maximum penalty, but he *would* do it. . . .' And, as his victim walked slowly and sadly away, he would chuckle: 'Bert unsettles 'em and I settle 'em.'

II

BUT Uncle Walter's Primitives, grand folk as they were, formed no more than a curtain-raiser to the glorious pageant of cricket. The illustrious actors who held the centre of the stage were the Yorkshire eleven of the period. A right-minded boy should back his own side and be patriotic rather than rational at such a stage of his life, but my partisanship stretched beyond all reason. To me these Yorkshire players were only 'a little lower than the angels'. Long before I ever saw one of them in the flesh, I knew them all as characters in a shining saga, a Romaunt of the White Rose, whose eternal troubadour was Uncle Walter. They were all heroes in an unending serial story.

I owned their photographs—Hirst, Rhodes, F. S. Jackson, Haigh, Denton and several others—printed on shiny cigarette cards given away with Ogden's Guinea Gold cigarettes. I acquired these cards at school through an elaborate system of barter in which marbles, horse-chestnuts and foreign stamps played their parts. I remember that I once swopped a live bee in a match-box for Lord Hawke.

The only characters comparable in my imagination with that Yorkshire side of mid-Edwardian days were Robin Hood's Merry Men or the Seven Champions of Christendom, about whom I had read with awed admiration in the pink-backed library of penny volumes called Stead's *Book for the Bairns*. My heroes were admirable because they were heroic. It was as simple as that. Their actions, as recounted by Uncle Walter, had the quality of Homeric deeds, far on the ringing plains of windy Troy.

George Hirst was burly, massive of shoulder, strong as a lion, a 'heart-and-soul' cricketer, if ever one was born. Rhodes was a bowler, smooth in action as the perfect machine, youthful and ruddy of countenance as the boy David, but even then a veteran in guile. They came from the same tiny stone-built village of Kirkheaton and their feats were fantastic, whether performed singly or in happy partnership. Had not the two of them dismissed a strong Australian team for 36 (repeat thirty-six) in that Birmingham Test match of 1902, in which England were robbed of overwhelming victory by rain and cosmic injustice? That England eleven which played at Birmingham, as knowledgeable men were to maintain for the next half-century, was the strongest that England ever fielded. And three of them were Yorkshiremen. In the tourists' very next match two of the three peerless ones—it was Hirst and Jackson this time—virtually obliterated the enemy. It was in a county match at Headingley, and on a pitch of the utmost treachery, that the deed was done. To be out for 36 was destruction; to be out for 23 was annihilation. (Hirst five for 9; Jackson five for 13.) Yorkshire, even after that, were left with 50 to make to win and were hard put to it to get them. Only one batsman reached double figures: this was T. L. Taylor, the present president of the county club. He made 11 runs in a supreme effort and when he was out, it looked for the moment as if Yorkshire would never be able to fight their way through, but at that moment there arose another dexterous defender with the romantic name of Irving Washington, who made only 9, but this was enough. I wish you could have seen how Uncle Walter, his umbrella stylishly gripped, showed the bold leg-hit with which Washington had put an end to Yorkshire's doubts and clinched a glorious victory. That leg-hit very nearly swept the marble clock off the mantelpiece and it would have been hard to explain to Aunt Martha that it was all Irving Washington's fault.

Alas for Irving Washington, he was never robust in health; his career was shining but short and, like his even more brilliant nephew, Roy Kilner, he died young. Uncle Walter's saga of 1902 included the other match of that year, a more glorious match even than the other two, perhaps the most glorious match in history; the Oval Test, Jessop's match in which England snatched a final victory by one wicket against all probability. Uncle Walter was a partisan, and would only have countenanced the pusillanimous motto: 'May the best team win,' in the sense allowed by W.G.: 'Well, ain't we the best team?' Nevertheless, he was as fair-minded as any genuine partisan could be. Yorkshire was his dwelling-place and heaven his destination and he may have honestly doubted whether there would be much difference. But he appreciated valour in his foes and, though this required greater sympathy and understanding, even in his allies. To Jessop he awarded fullest honours, though he reckoned Mr. Jessop would have to admit that both Jackson and Hirst had helped him a bit. To the stand for the unbroken last wicket which brought home final victory he gave all the story-teller's art and when he came abreast (magnificently if apocryphally) of Hirst's hoarse battle-cry, 'We'll get 'em in singles, Wilfred,' he gave to it the patriotic fervour of Henry the Fifth's address to the troops before Harfleur. Now let me make the only startling revelation in this unstartling volume. Almost exactly half a century after the event, I asked those two great English gentlemen about the immortal words. Mr. Rhodes was frankly doubtful as to whether the words had even been said and Mr. Hirst, perhaps more diplomatically, replied: 'Well, you know, at a time like that you never quite remember what you say...' It therefore seems likely that if George Hirst did not say the words, it was necessary that someone should have invented them. It is a solemn thought, and it may well be that Uncle Walter, as 'corroborative detail to enhance an otherwise bald and unconvincing narrative', invented them himself. But when I think that, I also recall how I first heard from his lips the story of the battle of Trafalgar. (He never once claimed to have been present.) And if I believe that Uncle Walter invented Hirst's signal, then I am forced to believe that he invented Nelson's signal, too.

He reserved his most vivid narration for Hirst's stupendous effort in the first innings. 'All honour to Mr. Jessop,' said Uncle Walter generously, 'and a grand finish it was an' all, but if George Hirst hadn't saved the follow-on in the first innings, Mr. Jessop could never have shone out in all his glory.' And then he would paint the picture of George Hirst standing at bay so dramatically that I saw him as Leonidas in the blood-drenched gap at Thermopylæ. And, after all, Leonidas had about three hundred Spartans with him. George Hirst had only one, by name Bill Lockwood. You would have thought from his mastery of detail that Uncle Walter had been to the Oval and watched every ball of this match. The truth is that at this stage of his life he had never been farther south than Bramall Lane, Sheffield. His narrative sprang from pure imagination—imagination reinforced by Old Ebor, that prince of cricket-writers, whose daily column in the *Yorkshire Evening Post* Uncle Walter regarded (and rightly) as the pure milk of the word. If I received it in pre-digested form, I was a lucky boy.

These heroes of ours were in my imagination so much larger than life that to see them for the first time on the field might have brought sad disillusionment. Not so. One of the Sankey hymns that Uncle Walter used to whistle had a quatrain:

> *Hark 'tis the voice of angels,*
> *Borne in a song to me*
> *Over the fields of glory,*
> *Over the jasper sea ...*

Over the fields of glory ... Who could fail to tremble with delight? I first saw George Hirst in the first county match I ever witnessed. This was at Headingley on Bank Holiday Monday, 1904, and I could write a solemn book—I think I could have written a book on the Tuesday—about the wealth of capacity (in Churchillian phrase) that lived in the twenty-two men of that match. Not all of them were great cricketers, though at least half of them were, which is a very high proportion for one game. All of them, however, were cricketing characters. I have not changed my opinion that Hirst, Rhodes and Jackson were the most powerful trio of all-rounders a county—or even a country—ever had at one time, while, on the other side, MacLaren, Spooner and Johnny Tyldesley were not merely the most formidable but the most attractive Nos. 1, 2 and 3 of their period. You might, according to your age and place of origin, prefer England's Hobbs, Sutcliffe and Hammond or Australia's Woodful, Ponsford and Bradman, but no mere county ever possessed such an illustrious triumvirate as the Lancashire of that time.

It was the first time I had ever been inside a large cricket

ground and I suppose, at ten, I ought to have shown a little
more sophistication, but I gazed out over the fields of glory
and gave myself wholly up to wonder—wonder at the noise,
which was like the murmur of the sea; at the size of the scoreboard, which was as much bigger than anything I had seen
before as it was smaller than the serial-story boards of Sydney
and Melbourne; at the refreshment booths, their shelves
stacked with myriad bottles of pop and mountains of twopenny
pork-pies and penny tea-cakes; and at the voice of the man who
sold score-cards, intoning as though it were a litany: 'I have
all on for one penny and the order of bowlers and batters.' He
made it even more delightful by pronouncing bowlers to
rhyme with schoolboy howlers.

The crowd seemed to me colossal and so it was. The attend-
ance on the three days, including Uncle Walter and myself,
was, as afterwards revealed by Old Ebor, 78,681, and the total
takings (shilling for Uncle Walter and sixpence for me) were
over £3,000. This was George Hirst's benefit match, granted
for what the soberest of cricket commentators called 'twelve
years of splendid service', and his reward was not only richly
deserved, but rich. The sum received was £3,703, which was,
and remained, a record for many years. (Roy Kilner's £4,016
in 1925 was the first total to break this record.) Since two world
wars, at least eight people, if not more, have doubled Hirst's
figure, three have trebled it and one has almost quadrupled it.
Good luck to all of them. But, speaking as a north country man,
with a reverent sense of the value of money, I would rather
have had the things that George Hirst's £3,703 could buy in
1904 than what £14,000 can buy now. Not that it matters to
a living soul.

It was a glorious morning on the Monday, but it had rained
all the previous Saturday and part of the Sunday and there was
no doubt that when MacLaren won the toss, his first thought
was: 'Ah, now we'll have the beggars on a drying pitch and
skittle 'em.' That was why we did not see one of the most
heartening sights in England (for a Lancashire man): Mac-
Laren and Spooner striding to the crease. Hornby and Barlow
were hymned in cricket's noblest verse; MacLaren and
Spooner, who, in strict fact, must have been far greater batsmen, have been celebrated in Cardus's glittering prose.

Of the two whom I now saw coming out to bat, one was
known to me through the reliable, if less distinguished, medium
of Uncle Walter, and the other was known to me by sight.
This was Harry Wilkinson, an amateur with a slightly crooked
nose who came from our own home town. At home, playing in
Yorkshire Council matches for the town team, he was a prolific
hitter of sixes; for the county side he played strictly to orders,
valuable in defence but unexciting to watch. His partner was
an authentic immortal, the Hon. F. S. Jackson, who the following year was to captain a triumphant England team against the
visiting Australians, win the toss five times and top the averages for both batting and bowling. (Those were the days when
you did not have to feel morally guilty if you received your
share of luck.) Jackson was a debonair fighter with a flair for
victory, who hit every ball hard, even in defence, and bowled
every ball fast and straight. He made you feel as Tennyson felt
about the Duke of Wellington, who 'never lost an English
gun'. Yet he, the great one, was the first to go, bowled by Willis
Cuttell, himself a renegade Yorkshireman. David Denton, the
gay cavalier with the cavalry moustache, came in next and,
alas, went soon. It was characteristic of this happy-hearted
cricketer that he should not stay long without scoring. You
could get him out, but you could not pin him down. Tunnicliffe came next and defence, as dictated by 'constraint and sad
occasion,' became the order of the day. Here was another
natural hitter who had disciplined himself into solidity. It was,
said Uncle Walter, an odd thing to see Tunnicliffe at No. 4
instead of No. 1.

That year had dissolved one of Yorkshire's goodliest opening
partnerships. Among those there have been at least three outstanding ones: Ulyett and Louis Hall, Brown and Tunnicliffe, Sutcliffe and Holmes. Sir Leonard Hutton, a greater individual artist than any of this handsome half dozen, was never
in his prime blessed with the perfect opening partner: in
Washbrook, for England, he came very near to it; in the county
arena, never. In my schooldays we never thought there could
be a more famous opening pair than Brown and Tunnicliffe:
Brown, the elegant stylist and inspired late cutter, Tunnicliffe,
the rocklike defender who was capable of tiring out the most
hostile bowling and completing his century at the end of the

day. Brown during the past eight years had played for England
eight times, and his 140 in Melbourne in 1894–95 was a shining contribution to victory in the rubber. Tunnicliffe never
played in a Test match, though he was in many ways a finer
opening batsman than many who have gone in first for England since. There were several reasons why Tunnicliffe gained
no England cap and among them were: A. E. Stoddart, Albert
Ward, A. C. MacLaren, Abel, C. B. Fry, Hayward and R. H.
Spooner. It was no disgrace to be not quite so good at exactly
the right time as any of these.

We did not see Brown that day, though we did not realize,
of course, that cricket would see him no more. He had broken
down after the first game of that season and later in the year
was to die of heart trouble at the age of thirty-five. His absence
was a loss, but we did not know of its sad permanence as we
watched Tunnicliffe and Harry Wilkinson steadily pull the
game round. No doubt the batting was slow, but if you are
fervently on the defending side, you do not think the defence
dull. For myself, I could not think of it in terms other than the
gallant defence of a beloved citadel. The attack was defied
and the hundred was up on the board—I had never seen such
a big board in my life—before the next wicket fell. I then
heard the loudest and happiest cheer I have ever heard. It rose
and swelled like a chorus from Handel. George Hirst, all Yorkshire packed into a single sturdy frame, was emerging from the
pavilion's shade into the sunshine and moving purposefully
out towards the crease. Every man and boy in their serried
ranks around the rails stood up and shouted. It was an instinctive act of homage towards the basic idea of Yorkshire; of Yorkshire stubbornness, Yorkshire courage and Yorkshire resource.
We did not know then that there was anything wrong in the
cult of personality. I still remember the sentence in which Old
Ebor of the *Yorkshire Evening Post* described Hirst's arrival at
the wicket as well as any lines from Milton or Keats I learned at
school at about the same time.

*The beneficiary stood for a moment, imperturbably fasten-
ing his glove.*

For a moment it was as though a king were gazing round in
benevolence upon his loyal subjects. Then resolutely, though
without ill-feeling, he set about the bowling. Almost at once

he lost his partner, and very soon he lost another, but he never looked like getting out. The phrase has become a cliché, but it had a meaning when it was first coined. George Hirst was not interested in the possibility of defeat. He did not defend forlornly, but attacked aggressively, and when Ernest Smith came out to join him, the pair of them batted as if the bowling had no sting whatever and it was a mere question of how many runs could be piled up in the day. Ernest was one of that devoted band of August schoolmasters—happily they survive to-day—who pack their boys off home and add a kind of academic gaiety to the month's cricket. Such schoolmasters of late years have been M. M. Walford, of Sherborne and Somerset, and John Dewes, of Rugby and Middlesex, and I will wager that Dewes played far more sparkling cricket for Middlesex in August than ever he did in his Cambridge days.

Ernest Smith took his cricket as he found it. He could defend like a lowered portcullis if Yorkshire were in serious trouble, but to-day he was in festive mood. Why should not a schoolmaster have fun on August Bank Holiday? After being missed before he had scored, to the accompaniment of about 30,000 gasps he went on batting like a charging cavalry leader. I do not remember how the scoring went; I only know that Hirst made 65 and that I thought it a tragedy when he was out. Ernest Smith advanced to within two runs of his century and was still hitting merrily away, in partnership with Lord Hawke, at the end of the day. Lord Hawke was, to complete my visit, the first peer of the realm I had ever seen. For me he did not need to wear a coronet. He was not so much a nobleman as an institution.

I did not see the finish of the match, which after the promise of a thrilling Yorkshire victory ended in a draw on the third afternoon. It did not dribble away, as many matches do nowadays. Hirst's bowling showed all the fire and purpose that his batting had displayed and Lancashire were forced to follow on, but from that moment Johnny Tyldesley, the most dazzling professional batsman of the day, fought back almost single-handed, scored a century and caused triumph to slip through Yorkshire's fingers. It was impossible for Uncle Walter to conceive the possibility of abandoning work to watch a cricket match two days in succession. Such a doubling of happiness was beyond the grasp of our imagination.

III

IT is indisputable, I think, that some of the best cricket ever seen was played in those years around the turn of the century and that the players of that time were the men of the Golden Age. Yorkshire and Lancashire, as I still maintain, were peopled by heroes and there were great men in other counties, too: the powerful and elegant K. L. Hutchings, of Kent, and his tall, slim, handsome young clubmate, Frank Woolley; Jessop, of Gloucestershire, greatest master of controlled hitting in history; the veteran Hayward and the young Hobbs, of Surrey, and with them the schoolboy of genius, J. N. Crawford; the frail but immensely talented P. F. Warner, of Middlesex, and B. J. T. Bosanquet, only begetter of the googly; Fry and Ranji, of Sussex, masters respectively of the classic and the exotic, two names that can never be omitted from the muster roll of the great; the Fosters of Worcestershire, H.K., R.E., the most brilliant of the lot, W.L., B.S., G.N., M.K. and N.J.A.; no wonder the county was often called Fostershire; from Somerset L. C. H. Palairet, still, after nearly sixty years, the model of all 'beautiful' batsmen, and Braund, an all-rounder worthy to play No. 6 in the 'perfect' eleven of 1902 and a slip-fielder even better, if such a thing were physically possible, than Tunnicliffe; from Leicestershire, J. H. King who, coming in as reserve, made two centuries in his first Gentlemen v. Players match, and Albert Knight, as steady a bat and as good a Methodist as Louis Hall; and that astonishing methuselite, Philip Mead, of Hampshire, who first played in 1906, toured Australia in 1911 and again in 1928. On the second tour he was greeted by an enthusiastic Hill-ite who shouted: 'What cheer, digger, I knew your father seventeen years ago.' An incomparable England eleven, with Dick Lilley of Warwickshire to keep wicket, could have been drawn from among these and there were players of quality enough to form second and third elevens hardly less gifted.

My main feeling during this period of education under Uncle Walter was one of fairly pure patriotism, modified, except when Yorkshire were in peril, by a genuine desire to praise famous men and to admit, except under pressure, that there were great men before, and might even be after, Hirst and Rhodes.

Not always did Yorkshire win the championship, but they seized it in cavalier fashion the year following Hirst's benefit when, with three men absent playing for England, the county were able to bring up sufficient reserves to fill their places worthily. In international affairs this was Jackson's year, the season of England's triumph under his captaincy. And Yorkshire did not suffer. When they came to their last vital match at Leyton, they found that they at least had to draw it. Thus it came about that they were faced with the need, all the third day, to keep alive after following on 400 runs behind. You may ask who the batsmen were who had reduced Yorkshire to such straits? They were F. L. Fane, Carpenter, the Rev. F. H. Gillingham and Charlie McGahey. And the bowler who forced them to follow on was J. W. H. T. Douglas. In that second innings Essex employed seven bowlers. Hirst batted five hours for 90, and that joyous hitter, Ernest Smith, subjected himself to more than academic discipline and remained at bay for the last hour of the day for none not out. Never was there a more devoted example of a self-denying ordinance.

After Jackson's year, Hirst's year. In 1906 Hirst performed the unbeatable and unrepeatable feat of scoring 2,180 runs and capturing 203 wickets. Cricket knows no higher act of sustained endurance. In spite of these superhuman efforts Yorkshire lost the championship, and lost it by one run. Their last match was played at Bristol, scene of Gloucestershire's hardest battles. It had been a grim fight all through, and when Yorkshire's last man, Arthur Ringrose, came in, eleven runs were still wanted. The man at the other end was that sturdy fighter, Hubert Myers, who was used to affairs of this kind. In a queer way the scene seemed to re-echo that even more dramatic scene at the end of the famous 'Ashes' match of 1882, when an earlier Yorkshire bowler went out in confidence to save the game and utterly lost it, leaving an infinitely better batsman than himself to carry out a bat he had had no chance to use. There is no record that Ringrose said: 'I couldn't trust Hubert'; indeed, he did far better than Ted Peate in that he managed to remain alive while Myers, by skill and cunning, scored nine. But then with two runs still wanted to win, Myers for once failed in his 'farming' and Ringrose, unhappy orphan of the storm, was left to face the assault alone. Jessop, a shrewd, hostile and dominating captain, took over the bowling himself and began the fatal over. The first ball would have flown away for four byes but for an acrobatic somersault by Jack Board. The third ball hit Ringrose on the pad and the appeal must have startled the orphans in the nearby home on Ashley Down. The umpire raised his finger and Gloucestershire had won the championship *for Kent*. It seemed to me (quite irrationally) a tragedy that the fate of so finely contested a match and of the year's championship should be decided by an l.b.w. decision, and my deepest feelings were lacerated by Old Ebor's wry comment: 'Mr. Jessop has received many congratulatory telegrams, some of them, *oddly enough*, from Kent . . .'

It took me years to forgive that *oddly enough*. Irony is not for the very young.

IV

ON the ground of our town club I saw, in Uncle Walter's company, an innings by Jessop in which he hit Wilfred Rhodes three times over mid-wicket and thence over the stand, which seemed to us an act of insensate profanity. Jessop's fury could have hurled Yorkshire to defeat if Schofield Haigh had not clean bowled him in full career. Gloucestershire instantly curled up and died, as though the heart had been cut out of them, as indeed it had. Then Yorkshire, who had trembled on the edge of ignominy as long as Jessop was in, won by 35 runs.

I also saw a drawn game against a strong Leicestershire eleven. In this match Rhodes made 122 in what would now be reckoned a fast time and showed those qualities which made him an ideal partner for Jack Hobbs. He possessed few of the more purely beautiful strokes; indeed, it was a maxim of his that the cut was not a business proposition, but on the leg-side he hit hard, often and with perfect safety. I also remember this match because I saw Albert Knight who, at a modest level, had been a hero of mine ever since I had followed (on the kitchen hearth-rug) the fortunes of Warner's conquering side in Australia four years before. When I saw him in person he was correct rather than heroic, but he justified his solidity by making Leicestershire's top score. Early on the first morning of the game I had the slightly incredible privilege of bowling at the nets to one of the Leicestershire players. He also sold me a bat.

which afterwards turned out to be cracked. Looking back over this distance of time I must set down naught in malice. Besides, Uncle Walter advanced me the five shillings.

The most exciting of all these games that I saw, except for a certain fierce Yorkshire *v.* Lancashire match which I have re-called elsewhere,[1] ended in a draw of the kind which plainly proves that drawn games need not be dull games. It was my first visit to the Park Avenue ground at Bradford, that pleasant arena with its back turned rather haughtily to the football pitch and its pavilion perched almost as high above the playing pitch as the ground is above the town. We descended on Brad-ford (by excursion train) on the Saturday; that is, on the third day. At first our attitude was fairly complacent. Yorkshire had led Middlesex on the first innings, neither of which we had seen, by over a hundred but less than 150 runs. Hirst had scored 90 and Rhodes had taken five wickets for 49, but they had not been able to make the enemy follow on and we had no doubt that in the pavilion they were reproaching themselves for this comparative failure. (In those days Yorkshiremen sub-jected themselves to harsh self-criticism when anything went less than dead right.) We watched some brisk batting by Rhodes and Hardisty and when Rhodes was out, cleverly caught and bowled by the Middlesex Australian, Tarrant, Denton came in to make the bowling look not merely easy, but silly. It seemed absurd to imagine that Denton could ever des-cend to a defensive stroke. He did not rush down the pitch to meet the ball, but hit it with fury when it arrived and always to one or other of the great open spaces. When he was batting fieldsmen seemed thin on the ground. Could there really be eleven of them? There were no flicks or tickles; the ball was pulled or driven with the full force of the bat. His score rose to 60-odd in a surprisingly short time and then Lord Hawke deemed it safe to declare.

All Bradford solemnly debated the problem. Middlesex had been set to get 270 to win in two and three-quarter hours. I would not argue that such a task would be impossible to-day. On a plumb pitch against weak bowling it might be attempted and achieved. But would any captain try it against a strong bowling side? Would you relish trying to get three hundred

[1] See *Cricket My Happiness.*

runs against Loader, Lock, Laker and the two Bedsers in three hours? Absurd. Yet Middlesex boldly essayed the impossible, against the deadliest bowling side in the country, and nearly brought it off.

They had a workmanlike rather than a brilliant start. Warner and James Douglas played at a rate which, by ordinary county standards, would have been fairly reckless to-day, but was slow by the clock. Only 72 in fifty minutes and slow-coach Warner was out!

'They'll never do it at that rate,' said Uncle Walter comfortably.

Middlesex's next two efforts to remedy the scoring rate met with defeat and soon four wickets were down. Nothing now seemed more certain than that Middlesex would have to struggle hard to secure a draw.

At this point Tarrant, coming in later than usual, joined Douglas. From that moment the game went crazy. The batsmen attacked almost every ball at sight. Douglas, quick and graceful; Tarrant, downright determined and aggressive. There are times when the best possible attacking side seems to lose its grip. At one moment the bowlers were on top; at very nearly the next they were conquered, subjugated. Those two batsmen scored almost as they liked. The armour-plated 'field' was pierced and riddled. Hirst, Rhodes and Haigh were the best trio of bowlers in the country, and they were reinforced that day by J. T. Newstead, from Richmond, who was to be honoured at the end of the season as one of the Cricketers of the Year. (One of the others was Jack Hobbs.) Yet for an hour and a quarter these four met their masters and at the end of that time Middlesex, so far from struggling for a draw, were sailing on the crest of the wave to victory. The spectators applauded the strokes with a courtesy mixed with misgiving. Their admiration was genuine, if tinctured with gloom. The batting was glorious, but did the gods realize that it was *against* us?

'Nay,' murmured Uncle Walter, as though protesting at the essential iniquity in heaven's sight of such a situation. '*Nay* . . .'

And then Douglas hit up a tremendous skyer into the region of long-on. It was going over the rails. No. The trim figure of David Denton was running along the boundary and, as the

ball came slowly curving down, the fieldsman's unerring judgment brought him into precisely the right place and the ball
went into his hands with the inevitability of a train entering
the Tube tunnel. A roar rent the skies and the Bradford skies
needed some rending. A moment later a swift return from
Hirst robbed Tarrant of his wicket, a penalty for excessive
backing-up.

You would have thought that now Middlesex would have
retired into their shell and exchanged attack for defence. But
no. Some divine madness descended on them. Douglas and
Tarrant had scored at a rate of over a hundred runs an hour.
Fifty were still needed and although there was less than half
an hour to go, they decided to try the impossible or perish. It
was a mad but magnificent gesture. The crowd, hitherto
glumly polite, rocked with excitement as Hirst had two men
caught at the wicket in one over. I remember the catches well,
because they were taken by the second-eleven stumper, a
young fellow called Watson, the great David Hunter being
for some reason absent. Bradford is not a city given to the
wilder emotions, but as the chances swung erratically to and
fro, emotion mounted swiftly. First Yorkshire looked certain
to win; then the game looked like settling into a sedate draw.
Douglas and Tarrant had pulled it round in the direction of
what might have been an easy victory. Now Hirst, hurling his
thunderbolts, had plunged the whole question back into the
melting-pot again. Here came Albert Trott, another Australian, that dark and saturnine figure, the only man who ever
hit a ball clean over the pavilion at Lord's. He scratched a
lucky single and then Hirst, who seemed to be everywhere at
once, flung down his wicket as Trott attempted what seemed
a perfectly safe second run and the crowd were on their feet,
cheering wildly.

'We've got 'em now,' said Uncle Walter, not excitedly but
with all the responsibility of a man who had now taken over
the cares of captaincy. Unhappily we had not got them. There
were only two wickets to get and ten minutes in which to get
them; the best bowlers in the world bowling their hearts out,
the keenest fielders crowding like terriers round a corn-
stack at threshing time. But the defence held. At one end was
J. T. Hearne, one of cricket's most numerous families. J.T. was

an England bowler, but no bat—except on that day; at the other end was C. M. Wells, another of those August school-masters, slight of build but imperturbable as the England rugger full-back he had been some years before. Every ball sent down jerked at my heart as though it had been attached to that organ with a bit of string. But even Hirst could not move them. As he began his last over, there was an authentic 'breathless hush'. Middlesex were 32 runs behind and here they remained. One ball after another struck Hearne's bat or person. There was a roar when the fifth ball struck his pad, but the bearded umpire never moved a finger.

The last ball went into Watson's gloves and all was over.

'Eh, lad,' said Uncle Walter, rising from his normal form of standard speech into the vernacular which he reserved for moments of profound emotion, *'tha's seen summat this day . . .'*

Half a century and two world wars have passed and the world is a different and a sadder place. It is both a pointless and a churlish thing to praise the old days at the expense of the new, though there are a number of things a man might reasonably have preferred to commercial television and the hydrogen bomb. In the limited field of cricket, England for the moment stands supreme and Surrey, with six county championships in their belt, may register a claim to be the finest county side of their own, or any other, period, though those of us who saw the Yorkshire sides at the turn of the cen-tury and their successors of the early 'twenties, will dispute the second claim, while freely admitting the first.

Many of the young cricketers of to-day claim my utmost admiration for their skill and their lack of self-consciousness. It is impossible not to be impressed by them. Yet, because of what I learned at the feet of Uncle Walter, and of my age at the sunny beginning of this century that has gone cold and bleak on us, I can never feel that anything will be quite the same again. It was a true poet (though a tramp) who said:

> *My world this day has lovely been—*
> *But not like what the child has seen.*

Nor can I ever believe that there ever were or will be any cricketers of such unexampled quality as those who fulfilled their destiny in the early nineteen-hundreds. One or two are living yet. I saw Sidney Barnes and Wilfred Rhodes at Lord's when England last played the West Indies there and I have a letter from Sir Pelham Warner in front of me as I write. For me those years formed an era of unbroken sunshine. (This can be disproved at once by the Meteorological Office or by a glance at *Wisden* for any year of the period.) But for me, in retrospect, the sun always shone. As adjured by the motto on the old sundial, I counted only the happy hours and those hours were happy indeed.

That minor poet and major punster, Thomas Hood, wrote some lines which, if not profound, were profoundly true and, to me at least, unbearably sad.

> *I remember, I remember,*
> *The fir trees dark and high;*
> *I used to think their slender tops*
> *Were close against the sky;*
> *It was a childish ignorance,*
> *But now 'tis little joy*
> *To know I'm farther off from heaven*
> *Than when I was a boy.*

Such was the stature of the cricketers of those days that for me they were indeed close against the sky. In a special individual sense they were *my* Hirst, *my* Rhodes, *my* Jackson. When I watched them, sitting solemnly on a hard wooden bench by Uncle Walter's side, I was nearer to heaven than I shall ever be. The sun was pure gold, the sky the colour of lapis lazuli, the turf a living green. An enchanted gleam plays and will play on them for ever, lighting in poignant recollection the heart-breaking beauty of days that are gone.

Index